The Land Between

The Land Between

Encounters on the
Edge of the Canadian Shield

Edited by Thomas F. McIlwraith
with The Land Between Circle

Published for
The Land Between Circle

Fitzhenry and Whiteside

Fitzhenry & Whiteside acknowledges with thanks the Canada Council for the Arts, and the Ontario Arts Council for their support
of our publishing program. We acknowledge the financial support of the Government of Canada through the
Canada Book Fund (CBF) for our publishing activities.

 Canada Council for the Arts   Conseil des Arts du Canada

 ONTARIO ARTS COUNCIL CONSEIL DES ARTS DE L'ONTARIO
50 YEARS OF ONTARIO GOVERNMENT SUPPORT OF THE ARTS
50 ANS DE SOUTIEN DU GOUVERNEMENT DE L'ONTARIO AUX ARTS

Library and Archives Canada Cataloguing in Publication
The land between : encounters on the edge of the
Canadian Shield / edited by Thomas F. McIlwraith.
Includes bibliographical references.
ISBN 978-1-55455-211-5 (pbk.)
1. Natural history--Canadian Shield. 2. Indians of
North America--Canadian Shield. 3. Canadian Shield--
Literary collections. I. McIlwraith, Thomas Forsyth, 1941-,
editor of compilation
QH106.L33 2013   508.0971   C2013-902727-0

Publisher Cataloging-in-Publication Data (U.S.)
McIlwraith, Thomas F.
The land between : encounters on the edge of the Canadian Shield / Thomas F. McIlwraith.
[173] p. : col. ill., photos. ; cm.
Included bibliographical references.
Summary: A collection of essays and stories exploring the flora, fauna, landscape, history, geology, literature and mythology of the
Land Between, one of Canada's undiscovered ecotones, which ranges from the southern edge of the Algonquin Dome
to the outskirts of Kingston, Ontario, and is home to the Algonquin First Nation.

ISBN-13: 978-1-55455-211-5 (pbk.)
1. Ontario – Guidebooks. 2. Canadian Shield. I. Title
917.13044 dc23   F1057.M345 2013

Text and cover design by Kerry Designs

Printed and bound in China by Sheck Wah Tong Printing Press Ltd.

To the memory of Peter Alley,
intuitive and dedicated proponent for The Land Between

The Land Between, Incorporated (2011), is a registered non-profit Canadian charity. Its goals are to conserve and enhance the distinct cultural and natural characteristics of the region featured in this book. This mandate is achieved through education and research programs, and also by joint ventures with corporations, municipalities, and NGOs. The Corporation seeks to increase public awareness by exploring ideas and sharing results in regular seminars and workshops, for both adults and youth. The Land Between Council, which is the governing body, operates in a traditional Native Talking Circle, and is open to interested individuals. For more information please visit www.thelandbetween.ca.

The Land Between book was an idea brought forward by Thomas McIlwraith as a way of accessing and assembling impressions based on experiences, history, cultural orientation and scientific knowledge in the form of memoirs, stories and photographs and to present these in a portfolio publication that would communicate the diversity and array of relationships that exists in concurrence with the mosaic nature of this ecotone, in turn providing readers with an integral if not visceral curiosity, experience and appreciation of this dynamic landscape.

Foreword

James Bartleman

I grew up in The Land Between in the 1940s with a Native mother and white father. When I was a boy, I had a newspaper route delivering the *Toronto Daily Star* to some fifty customers spread out over some three miles in the village of Port Carling in Muskoka. Friday night was the highlight of the week. That was when I made my collections and had a chance to talk to the village elders. They were men and women in their seventies and eighties. All had been born before the turn of the 20th century to pioneer parents, mainly from the Old Country. They fed me hot chocolate and peanut butter cookies and told me of their early years in the district. They said their parents had read advertisements in British newspapers promising free land to British subjects prepared to pioneer in Muskoka, a place no one had heard of. All they had to do, they were told, was to clear the trees off the land and start planting wheat and oats in the deep, rich soil and soon, everyone would be well off.

After arriving in Muskoka and taking up their land grants, these newcomers discovered a different reality. The soil was thin and acidic, the blackflies and mosquitoes unbelievable, roads nonexistent or almost impassable; there were no doctors and the nearest grist mill was twenty miles away. But this first generation was not deterred in the new world. They found that if they worked together they could cope, and they soon had logging and house and barn-bees organised. Then the government dredged the river and built a wharf at Port Carling and regular steamer service from Gravenhurst soon followed. Tourists from Toronto and Pittsburgh started coming to fish and hunt and admire the scenery. These early adventurers needed places to stay, so the pioneers turned their farmhouses into guest houses. A tourism industry soon sprang up that provided the second generation with the kind of good living that had eluded their parents.

No one, however, wanted to talk about the Native people their parents had first encountered in Muskoka. And, as a respectful boy, I didn't ask them how the government of the day expelled a thriving Native community to make room for them. This community was called Obajewanung, consisting of some sixty people living in twenty log cabins with barns and fields. I also never asked why the pioneers had plowed over the graves of the ancestors and housed their pigs and cattle in the Native log cabins. And I never mentioned the petition addressed to the Crown by the Chief and people in January, 1862, pleading, in vain, to be allowed to remain in their homes and on their lands.

Father, this place is beautiful in our eyes and we cannot leave it. Many winters have passed since we settled here and began to cultivate our gardens. We have good houses and large gardens where we raise much corn and potatoes. Our children have grown up here and cannot make up their minds to go to a new place. We live by hunting and taking furs—and our hunting grounds are all near here. We hope you will grant the wish of your Red Children, and do it soon, because the whites are coming in close to us and we are afraid your surveyors will soon lay out our land into lots.

Things have changed slowly since, and today, much greater attention is being given to Native history and to the contributions that Native Canadians have made to the development of Canada. I am happy to see that this wonderful book celebrates the contributions of all Canadians, non-Native and Native, to our shared home in The Land Between.

Introduction: A Storehouse of Biodiversity in the Land Left Over

Peter Alley

There is an unusual natural heritage system in Ontario. It stretches from the southeast corner of Georgian Bay to the vicinity of Kingston, lying between the northern forests of the Canadian Shield and the farms of the Great Lakes Lowlands. Call it The Land Between. Here is a mosaic transition zone high in biodiversity, with a geological core of granite barrens—the exposed bedrock borders of the Shield—and limestone plains covered widely in mixed woodland.

For generations The Land Between has been an overlooked landscape, and for a variety of reasons. Much of it is bare rock or very thin soil. It is sparsely settled and remains in a largely natural state. The Canadian Shield and the Great Lakes Lowlands, on either side, are vastly larger by comparison and have drawn most of our attention for almost two centuries. The natural values of The Land Between and, indirectly, its social values, stem from its distinctive mixture of wetlands, shallow water bodies and a core of open patches of bare rock. Ecologists identify it as a unique mosaic transition zone—an ecotone—with links to other important Ontario landscapes, and celebrate its rich biodiversity and delicate soil and water system. The social values are its mute record of Ontario history, its home for those who love its ruggedness and its role as a summer home or refuge for countless city-dwellers. It is a matchless advantage for Ontario citizens to have access to a wilderness like The Land Between.

The Land Between is a complex, irregularly-shaped strip of land about 240 kilometres long and from 20 to 40 kilometres or more in width, formed by fundamental transitions in geology, elevation, and plant hardiness. Geologically, the core is two strips, one of Precambrian period and the other of Ordovician age. Each is essentially bare, with less than 15 centimetres average depth of soil cover. The core lies between two kinds of till deposits, minerals to the north and glacial ones to the south. Water and soil tend to be acidic in the granite barrens, while in the limestone plains, marble outcrops and the southern glacial tills are alkaline. Alkaline and acidic conditions mix in the countless rivers flowing through. An increase in elevation from about 200 metres above sea level in the farmlands to the south, up the slope northward onto the Algonquin Dome, at an elevation of about 400 meters, almost coincides with this geological transition. In turn, plant hardiness Zone 4b (a terminology familiar to gardeners) matches with this sloping geological core, marking climatic change between Zone 5a (warmer and wetter) of the Great Lakes Lowlands and Zone 4a (cooler and drier) of the Shield. Working together, these features make The Land Between a distinguishable transi-

This essay was written in 2006, months prior to Peter Alley's death. It was intended for an audience of scientists focused on ecotone research. The editor has adapted it for publication here, incorporating Alley's early and evolving thoughts regarding cultural ecology.

The eroded edge of the limestoneabove is within two kilometres of the granite barrens pictured in the right-hand view. The flat top of the high granite hill is a remnant of the very flat Ordovician peneplain on which limestone was deposited. Mellon Lake Conservation Reserve, south of Kaladar, Lennox and Addington County. (photos courtesy of Dugald M. Carmichael)

tion zone and an identifiable entity in itself.

The prevailing view among natural scientists prior to the 1980s was that an ecotone was merely a composite of features sandwiched between homogeneous ecological units, and difficult to describe and classify. But that kind of residual categorization may be misleading if the ecotone can be understood to have its own ecological structure, functions and rate of change. A mind focused on the search for homogeneity might overlook heterogeneity as an ecological value, and that seems to have been the case for The Land Between. Since the 1980s, however, scholars have come to view ecotones in a more enlightened way. Wrote one researcher:

> *[Ecotones] are recognized as being dynamic components of an active landscape, frequently playing significant roles in supporting high levels of biological diversity as well as primary and secondary productivity, modulating flows*

of water, nutrients, and materials across the landscape, providing important components of wildlife habitat, and acting as sensitive indicators of global change.

(Risser, 1995, 324).

While initially recognized for their great biological diversity, ecotones are today increasingly appreciated for their high levels of cultural diversity too. Thinking about The Land Between in both biological and human terms simultaneously marks a significant step forward in our understanding of the meaning of landscape and place.

The Land Between ecotone is a mosaic, not a blend. The parts are a jumble of identifiable pieces; think chunky Irish stew, not purée. This characteristic distinguishes it from the more homogeneous neighbouring landscapes on either side. In a stretch of granite no more than ten kilometres in length one may encounter nearly bare metamorphic rock ridges (much of it gneiss) divided by trenches filled with swamps, marshes, bogs, some forest, small creeks and narrow shallow lakes. It is all in low relief, with lateral connections

9

frequently occurring along faults. This is in every sense a mosaic. The variety of ecosystems in the limestone plains is less pronounced, yet there, too, a noticeable internal mosaic of alvars, wetlands, and even small moraines is frequently visible. Strips and stepping stones of limestone pavements often extend into the southward edge of the granite, and pockets of thicker tills and lacustrine deposits are scattered much further northward.

The surface geology is the foundation for the biodiversity of The Land Between landscape. Biodiversity is valued as a sign of the health of the natural heritage in an area, and worthy of every effort at preservation. In mosaic ecotones we can expect to find a greater range of types of biodiversity than in other places, and such is the case in The Land Between. Genetic diversity—variety within a species—may be important when a species is under stress, such as at the edge of its range. Diversity between species may include not only a measure of the simple number of species present, but also their abundance. Community or ecosystem diversity—that is, the number and density of ecosystems (swamps, bogs, alvars, etc.)—results in increases in species diversity. We may also think of regional or landscape diversity when contemplating a mosaic transition zone. The Land Between appears to be unusually important for Ontario in all of these dimensions, a fact affirmed by field observations. Birds abound, signalling heightened diversity of all kinds. As many as 500 or 600 species of vascular plants may be represented within close proximity. The Land Between is the northern limit for some species and the southern limit for others; and contains Atlantic Coastal Plain and Prairie species in patches and species at risk. All this adds to the variety.

The Land Between is one of several major bands of landscape in Ontario that serve as links among natural spaces. Where they touch, species interact, promoting survival and diversity. A benefit of public recognition of The Land Between as an ecotone landscape is the opportunity to apply formal pressure to close significant gaps. At its west end lies the Georgian Bay Littoral Biosphere Reserve. At its east, about 40 kilometres north of Kingston, The Land Between runs into the Frontenac Arch, a corridor of the Shield that crosses the St. Lawrence River to the Adirondack Mountains. Corridors to the Oak Ridges Moraine and Algonquin Park may also be defined.

Ecological diversity begets cultural diversity, and The Land Between is an economic and cultural amenity of great significance for all Ontarians. City folk and residents in towns up to two hours away by car—the Greater Toronto Area, Barrie, Peterborough, Kingston and Ottawa—are the primary beneficiaries. Few metropolitan areas in the world have anything approaching this sort of open space so close. Tourist resorts and services to summer residents are central to the economies of many towns. Cottages are the dominant settlement type, and "cottage country" is an apt term for describing large parts of The Land Between. In many municipalities, seasonal residents outnumber permanent ones substantially, and for almost everyone, recreation is the reason for being there. Some forestry takes place, and a little trapping; farming once was prominent but now is all but gone. A variety of minerals are extracted in the eastern parts and quarries are widespread. Much of The Land Between that once was cleared of trees has grown back to a state close to wilderness, leaving a chapter of Ontario history written in the landscape, but fading steadily.

Many economic and social activities today depend on maintaining and enhancing the natural history of The Land Between. That attitude is to be encouraged, for everywhere this ecotone is vulnerable, and misguided use, or overuse, could be disastrous. Many rivers flowing into Lake Ontario and Georgian Bay rise in the granite barrens, which are laced with small lakes and creeks. These must be free to collect the rapid surface runoff from bare granite and thin mineral tills, but do little processing of groundwater. The limestone plains, being more porous, store and process groundwater to some extent, but not nearly so much as the deeper tills farther south. It's a fragile setting. Rare, threatened and endangered species make their home in The Land Between; that is typical of diversified areas. Here one may find southern twayblade orchid, prickly pear, loggerhead shrike, five-lined skink (Ontario's only lizard), the eastern Massasauga rattlesnake and eastern hognose snake. Many more species live fragile lives at the edge of their normal habitats. Southern ones at their northern limit include white oak, butternut, Virginia waterleaf, large-flowered bell-wort, willow flycatcher, and yellow-throated vireo. Among northern ones at their southern limit are jack pine, wolf, bear, and moose.

The Land Between may indeed seem at first blush to be land left over, of little natural history of heritage consequence, Yet, look again, and see that it is a storehouse of biodiversity, a place where strangers meet and unlikely combinations occur, a land for celebration and careful stewardship in which science and society share and learn.

Burleigh Falls

A Note from the Editor

Thomas F. McIlwraith

I first became aware of The Land Between while riding a ski lift near Orangeville. It would have been a Saturday morning in January, probably about 1998, and my downhill skiing companion at Caledon Ski Club that day was musing about the decline of privacy on his cottage lake off in Muskoka or Haliburton or somewhere in that direction. People with development plans were threatening his sanctuary. I listened sympathetically, and probably entered the occasional fatuous remark, if only to indicate that I was still listening. It all seemed very remote and, besides, our two minutes were up. That was the length of time it took to reach the top of the lift, and off we skied.

Barely ninety seconds later we reconverged in the lift line, boarding the ski lift once again. And then the conversation, or rather my companion's monologue, resumed. That downhill skiing break had come at a comma—certainly not a full stop—and it was developing into a rant. *What could be done? Does no one listen? There are plants, and wildlife, and ecosystems, all at risk. Purple loosestrife. Duckweed. Motor boats with water-skiers. Portable stereos.* And then our two minutes were gone.

Next time up I took a chance and interjected thoughts about land surveys and derelict farms on overgrown pastures. The following trip it was about alvars and heritage houses; one time it was summer camps. Always these conversations were laced with talk of public and private costs, grant applications, and volunteerism. It never stopped, and over several years I became absorbed by what my fellow skier, Peter Alley, was calling "The Land Between." With enthusiasm and determination, Peter was on to a splendid cause, and his spirit was infectious.

I learned all this about The Land Between through those little interrupted snippets, with solitary, downhill moments given over, again and again, to reflection and preparation for the next uphill sound bite. The forty-six stories in this anthology remind me of those wonderful and illuminating narratives I heard on the chair lift: essays that may be read in a few minutes, followed by contemplation of an underlying message, and then on to something quite different. You may feel almost bombarded by these prose-and-image fragments, and wonder at their seeming randomness, but I hope that you will gradually pull them together. These accounts are intended to invite you, repeatedly, to sit up in surprise, and to draw you into this wonderful region of Ontario—The Land Between—so little recognized as a coherent unit. This book is indeed one modest response to Peter's love and passion for this land.

Thinking back through this introductory experience, I now see the irony. There we were, skiing on the Niagara Escarpment, while lamenting the impact of recreation throughout the Shield fringe. Peter recognized this apparent contradiction as well, and fully understood that The Land Between flourishes today in large part because it provides so many recreational opportunities. He saw the threats, but believed in The Land Between as a lived-in place, not a museum. People using it must be encouraged to derive their greatest pleasure by doing so sensitively. Peter Alley thought of himself as a steward of a land he loved, always keen to steer its change in a direction that will honour its natural diversity far into the future.

* * *

I like stories.

Every building, every streetscape, every farmstead, every wood lot, every marsh, every lake, every rocky outcrop, and every individual in The Land Between has a story to tell, and each speaks freely if you care to listen.

All these voices and all these subjects are current, for everything in The Land Between is current just by its very existence today. But each one is intrinsically old as well. A frame house, a lakefront, a personality, a painting, a memoir, a wetland, a rock carving: every subject induces thoughts about the past and about the processes that connect earlier times with the present and project life onward into the future. Witnessing decline may be met with despair or indifference, yet clinging to a faded, non-functional element of an obsolete era is a doomed enterprise. Rather, landscape appreciation and ecological sensitivity arise when we can read the story of evolved change. Using a barn timber as a fence post tells us about changing farm practices; a new wheelchair ramp on an old Victorian town house speaks about how we deal with today's health issues. Celebrate that opportunity to understand social change by reading today's recognizable elements, irreversibly altered for survival. *The Land Between* is part of that celebration of human creativity.

Stephen Leacock (an old Land Betweener himself, from Orillia) once related his surprise at suddenly realizing that "the old grave that stood among the brambles at the foot of our farm was history." This was Leacock's "wow" moment, and my direction to the writers here was to offer readers such moments of revelation in their chosen subjects. I am confident that each reader will be drawn up short by some of these surprises. Did you know, for instance, that earthworms were not native to North America? I am equally certain that readers may also say, from time to time, "I knew that, and I thought everybody did." We all have our experiences and common knowledge, and get (and give) pleasure in sharing them through storytelling. *The Land Between* is an exploration of peoples' encounters with the landscape, and the questions—and not necessarily the answers—such exploration awakens.

Reading this book is a way of slipping unobtrusively through the countryside. It is a way of learning, and appreciating. Our intention is to encourage readers who may not have had the opportunity to wander the rear of Hastings County on a Thursday morning in May—and what a privilege that is—to begin to see that, with no more than the gentlest of nudges, there is much to discover, much to share. The Land Between is a place of endless cultural and physical diversity.

This whole exercise may seem impressionistic, vague, and certainly random. Why is there no essay about blueberries, or mahogany motor launches, or Sandford Fleming? Why bother with Jean Sibelius, or uranium, or Otto Jacobi, or roads with three ruts? Why should readers have to act on their own if they wish to find out more about a stonemason in Haliburton or a First Nation at Curve Lake? All worthwhile questions, and all inviting the same response: that there is no limit to the subject matter that might foster awareness of The Land Between. But neither is there any doubt that the ideas that indeed have been incorporated into this book are, I believe, sufficient to stir the juices of inquisitiveness and surprise lurking within each of us. And that is our goal.

The Land Between is a collaborative effort. This project took shape in 2007, at a time when "The Land Between" was an expression adopted by a largely informal gathering of like-minded individuals under the umbrella of two land trusts: the Kawartha Heritage Conservancy and The Couchiching Conservancy. Following Peter Alley's death in the last week of 2006, Leora Berman took charge of keeping alive the spirit of his initiative by installing a vision to celebrate and communicate the full bio-cultural story of the land, and from that arose the "fifty-scenes book" project, as we optimistically dubbed it. Well, forty-six comes close, and that number would have been beyond reach had it not been for the superb contributions of Alan Brunger, Brian Osborne and John Wadland, who joined in as supportive editorial advisors. They provided names of potential contributors, vetted manuscripts, offered cautionary advice, and were always at the other end of the phone or email when needed. Kerry Plumley's skill as book designer shows on every page.

The Land Between has come together through the involvement of some forty authors, and I am eternally grateful for their wide ranging ideas and imagination. I generally had an idea about what subjects each writer might tackle, but thank goodness I had the good sense to leave the final decision in their hands. How else would I have discovered A.Y. Jackson's poignant experience on Georgian Bay, or a pair of dogs aboard a canoe in a snowstorm on Cranberry Lake? I had no idea how much there was to learn about a region of Ontario, and having eye-opening moments one after another over many months has been one of the delights of this enterprise. Through email I have acquired a broadened circle of colleagues, many of whom I have never met. Our discussions have been a stimulus and a privilege. Some day I hope to greet these forty co-authors face-to-face to acknowledge, once again, their splendid contributions.

Speculative and creative minds invariably must face the reality that some conjectures may turn out to be off the mark or lead us down the proverbial garden path. To all—readers and authors alike—I say, take solace in the words of James Joyce: "A man of genius makes no mistakes. His errors are volitional and are the portals of discovery." We all are, collectively, that genius, and the mistakes we make invariably lead to new understanding. In the end what we have written here about The Land Between is our responsibility. It is never truly definitive, but I hope we may be closer to it than when we started out.

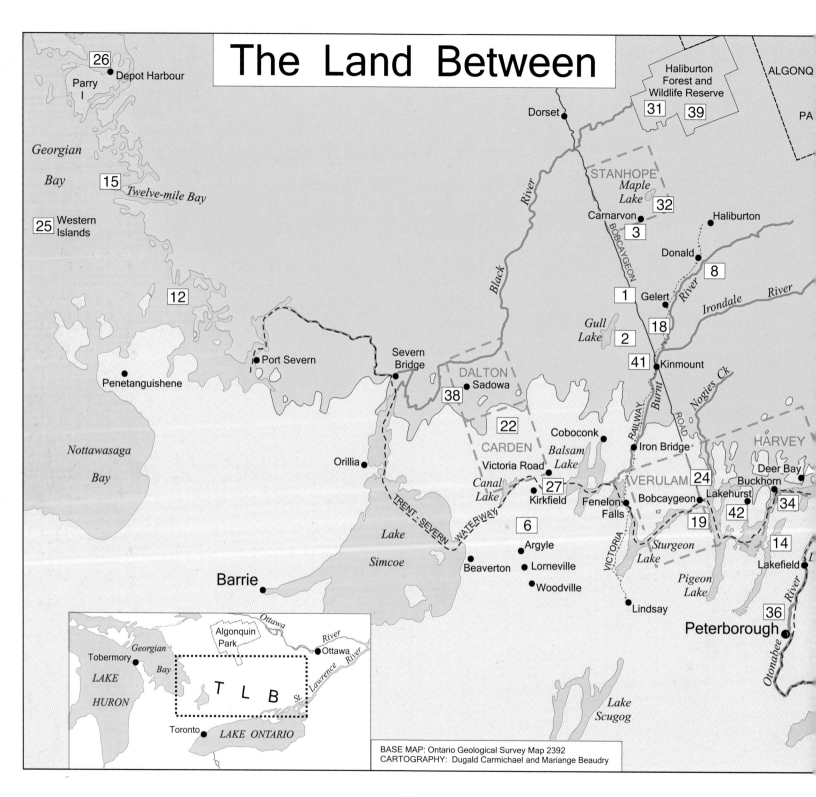

The Land Between

26 Parry I • Depot Harbour

Georgian Bay

15 — *Twelve-mile Bay*

25 Western Islands

12

Nottawasaga Bay

ALGONQ
PA

Haliburton Forest and Wildlife Reserve

31   39

Dorset •

STANHOPE

Maple Lake

32

Carnarvon •
3

Haliburton •

Donald •
8

1   Gelert •

18

Gull Lake

2

41   • Kinmount

Irondale River

BOBCAYGEON

Black River

• Port Severn

Severn Bridge

DALTON
38   • Sadowa

22

CARDEN

• Coboconk

Balsam Lake

• Iron Bridge

• Orillia

Victoria Road •

Canal Lake

27   • Kirkfield

24

HARVEY

Deer Bay •

VERULAM

Bobcaygeon •   Lakehurst •
19   42

34

Fenelon Falls •

Sturgeon Lake

14

• Penetanguishene

6

Lake Simcoe

• Argyle

• Beaverton   • Lorneville

• Woodville

Barrie

• Lindsay

Pigeon Lake

• Lakefield

36

Peterborough

Nogies Ck

Burnt River

RAILWAY   ROAD

VICTORIA

Otonabee River

Lake Scugog

Tobermory •

Georgian Bay

Algonquin Park

• Ottawa
Ottawa River

St. Lawrence River

LAKE HURON

T L B

Toronto •   **LAKE ONTARIO**

BASE MAP: Ontario Geological Survey Map 2392
CARTOGRAPHY: Dugald Carmichael and Mariange Beaudry

16

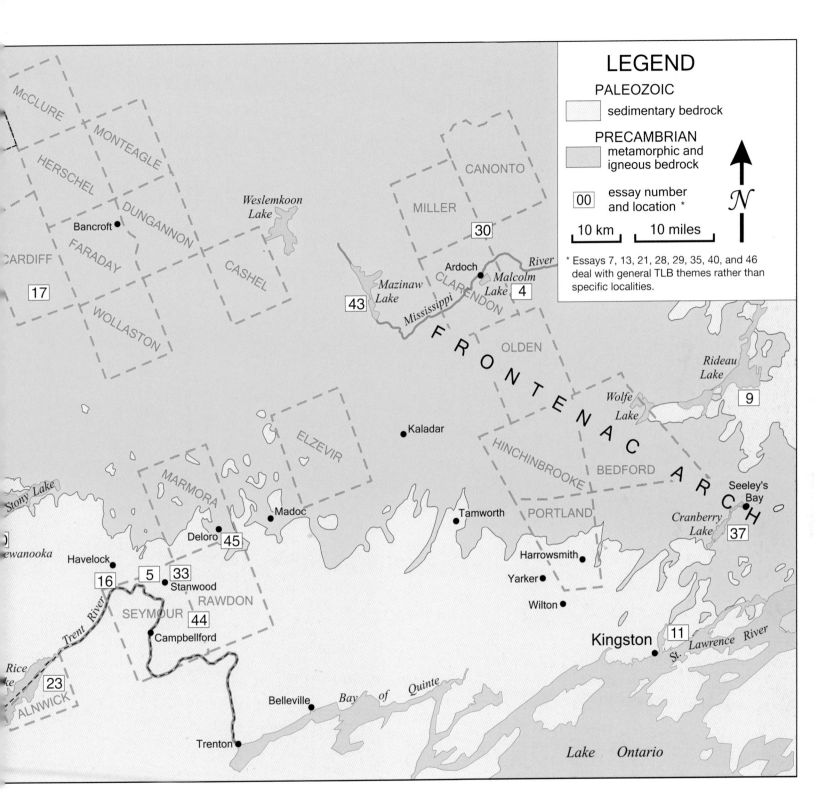

LEGEND

PALEOZOIC
sedimentary bedrock

PRECAMBRIAN
metamorphic and igneous bedrock

00   essay number and location *

10 km   10 miles

N

* Essays 7, 13, 21, 28, 29, 35, 40, and 46 deal with general TLB themes rather than specific localities.

McCLURE

MONTEAGLE

HERSCHEL

DUNGANNON

Weslemkoon Lake

Bancroft

CARDIFF

FARADAY

CASHEL

17

WOLLASTON

CANONTO

MILLER

30

Ardoch   River

Mazinaw Lake   Malcolm Lake

CLARENDON

4

43

Mississippi

FRONTENAC ARCH

OLDEN

Rideau Lake

Wolfe Lake

9

Kaladar

ELZEVIR

HINCHINBROOKE

BEDFORD

Seeley's Bay

MARMORA

Stony Lake

Madoc

Tamworth

PORTLAND

Cranberry Lake

37

Deloro   45

ewanooka

Havelock

16   5   33

Stanwood

RAWDON

Harrowsmith

Yarker

SEYMOUR

44

Wilton

Campbellford

Kingston

11

St. Lawrence River

Trent River

Rice ke

23

ALNWICK

Belleville   Bay of Quinte

Trenton

Lake Ontario

1. Heartbreak along the Bobcaygeon Road

Neil S. Forkey

By the middle of the 1850s, the Government of the Province of Canada was facing a serious land problem. Owing to the scarcity of cheap farmland in Canada West (roughly southern Ontario today), prospective settlers and emigrants too often were giving up on the region and moving onward to the American midwest. The best locations along the St. Lawrence Lowlands-Great Lakes corridor had long since passed into private hands. The Canadian government needed to find more farmland, but where? Directing would-be settlers into The Land Between, including the southernmost Canadian Shield, seemed to offer a solution and, as a result, between 1856 and 1866 the province laid out and opened some twenty colonization roads, establishing access to Crown land for settlement and farm making. The Bobcaygeon Road, leading from its namesake village northeast of Lindsay across the Shield front and onward to Haliburton County, was one of these.

Few might have imagined that a farming community could take root north of Bobcaygeon. That rugged area was apparently the exclusive domain of lumbermen. Here, in 1856, the Boyd Company was cutting upwards of 20,000 feet of lumber each day (equivalent to twelve or fifteen simple frame storey-and-a-half farmhouses), and its land acquisitions—invariably leases—were growing. Yet amid such destructive (if lucrative) activity, and despite the roughness of the terrain and the short growing season, by 1859 more than 300 pioneers had arrived to take up

Once settlement opened up in Iowa and Manitoba in the Confederation era, it is hard to imagine anyone choosing to farm along the Bobcaygeon Road. For those who persisted this is how it looked in the 1910s. (photo from Howe and White, Commission of Conservation, 1913)

residence as landowners along the Bobcaygeon Road. For the Boyds and other lumberers, local residents were a welcome addition to the landscape because they could supply the forest operations with food and labour. Furthermore, these roads enhanced lumber activities during the winter.

It rapidly became apparent, however, that the land along the Bobcaygeon Road could not sustain family settlement. Few families ventured onto the frontier for this reason, and today's landscape betrays as much. Single men, or groups of men, occupying the same land-holding, were rather more the norm. Through the winters they would work in the lumber camps in order to earn hard cash and buy supplies. They rented out their draft animals, both horses and oxen, for hauling timber. This seasonal work was an appropriate short-term strategy, but not one that would sustain a permanent community. These "pretend" settlers had no intention of clearing the land for field crops. Rather, their plan was to cut the pine growing on their lots, sell it to local companies, and then abandon the very holding on which they had chosen to be owners. The whole procedure was terribly wasteful and fires in the debris were common. John Langton, a long-

time local resident on Sturgeon Lake who later became Canada's public auditor, criticized the plan as early as 1862. The Province of Canada was thoroughly displeased. Here it was conducting land surveys, hiring colonization agents, and constructing a road, all for the purpose of establishing and retaining population, and this outcome was not happening.

The Bobcaygeon Road as a conduit for settlement ultimately failed. By 1911, after decades of decline, the population in the townships along the route numbered only about 4,800. A century later the rural, non-recreational population in the area was a small fraction of that. Those residents who stayed did so only with great difficulty and no small degree of will power. Their lands had been denuded of prime forest and were agriculturally marginal. In the Bobcaygeon Road experiment some overly zealous administrators believed that inhospitable lands could be brought under cultivation, much like settlements elsewhere throughout southern Ontario. The stark reality was, however, that the environment of The Land Between circumscribed settlement even more than it welcomed it. ■

2. Independence and Freedom: Sibelius and Lismer

John Parry

For people who live elsewhere, The Land Between can signify independence and freedom, as it has for so many people in my life. My parents spent much of the summer before I was born in "Bayview," a lovely old cottage on the harbour in Penetanguishene; my father's grandfather Louis Jacob Breithaupt of Berlin (later Kitch-ener) had purchased the property in about 1881. Louis had married Emma Devitt of Waterloo, and the Devitts loved the work of the great Finnish composer Jean Sibelius. *Finlandia* (1899) immortalized that northern land, with its wilderness, lakes, trees, and long, hard winters—so like Canada—and helped free Finland from Russia.

The Skinny Dip *was painted by Arthur Lismer in 1915 to fit over the porch door of a cottage on Georgian Bay. It now hangs in a special room in the National Gallery in Ottawa designed to recreate that setting. (courtesy National Gallery of Canada)*

That anthem became part of my life very early, long before my encounter with The Land Between. My father's sister used to tell me that my cousin Susan Devitt would play *Finlandia* on the piano for Uncle Frank, who would always cry. When my maternal grandparents gave my family their 78-rpm records in the early 1950s, the discs included Sibelius's stirring strains.

Finlandia so moved Susan Devitt's brother, Ed, that he set words to it. Four verses of *Maker of Men* became the camp hymn at two boys' summer camps in Haliburton: Comak, on Lake St. Nora near Dorset, and Kilcoo, on Gull Lake near Minden. We campers sang it there, standing near the tall evergreens and beside the lake, while someone lowered the Canadian red ensign each evening— "as sinks the sun beneath the western sky."

I realize now that that setting strikingly resembles the wilderness of Finland. Ed Devitt harnessed Sibelius's theme to evoke the awe and responsibility that we humans can feel before the magic, majesty, and mystery of The Land Between and its origins beyond memory. The history of Kilcoo Camp, published in 1999 by its long-time director John Latimer, carries the evocative title *Maker of Men*.

Scandinavia and The Land Between converge also in the art world. I think of Roald Nasgaard's *The Mystic North: The Symbolist Landscape Painters of Northern Europe and North America, 1890–1940* (1984)—one of my most exciting projects as a copy editor. Finnish artists Akseli Gallen-Kallela and Pekka Halonen and Canada's Group of Seven artists and Emily Carr capture the sublime power of lakes, trees, and climate. At least one counterpart of theirs added a further dimension: swimming, even the timelessness of skinny-dipping. The Norwegian Edvard Munch, on holiday on the Baltic coast, in 1907 painted the naked *Male Bathers*.

Many a family photo album from The Land Between I imagine portrays bathers *au naturel*, but few Canadian landscape artists have ever included people swimming. One exception is Arthur Lismer who, in 1915, created *The Skinny Dip*, a mural for the MacCallum-Jackman cottage on Go-Home Bay, in which stylized figures swim and dive naked from a rock. It now graces the National Gallery of Canada in Ottawa.

For me, thoughts of The Land Between and the escape that beautiful region offers can still evoke both feelings of the sublime—lakes, rocks, and trees, Sibelius and his stirring ode to independence— and memories of the simple pleasures of swimming and diving naked in the water "whose surface," to paraphrase the old prayer, "is perfect freedom." ∎

3. Dishing the Dirt on Soil

Nathan Basiliko

Soils sustain life on land, a role that extends far beyond simply serving as the rooting medium for plants. Except for carbon and oxygen from the air, nearly all of the fifteen or more elements essential for plant growth must come from the soil. Soils are arguably home to the greatest biodiversity on Earth, yet they remain among the most complex and least understood parts of our environment. The Land Between is testament to this diversity. Around Lindsay lie fertile soils in areas of glacial river and lake deposits. Along the eighty-kilometre span of Highway 35 northward to Carnarvon there occurs a quick transition to the acidic, shallow, rocky soils of the largest granite outcrop in the world—the mysterious, and sometimes notorious, Canadian Shield.

The transition of soil types is undoubtedly one of the major reasons for The Land Between being a recognized ecotone, but regional climate patterns also play a role. Cooler temperatures prevail northward, away from the lower elevations and moderating effects of the Lake Ontario plain. Those cooler air masses cannot hold as much moisture in the Haliburton highlands, leading to more precipitation. It is a complicated mix of soils and climate, supporting northerly elements of the Carolinian forest in some places, and the southerly extent of boreal species elsewhere. These conditions collectively create the unique wealth of plant, animal, and microbial biodiversity in the area.

Soils may represent millions of years of formative influences, but in The Land Between this time frame is severely truncated. The Pleistocene deglaciation, which was still occurring as recently as 11,000 years ago, has left us with young soils, commonly shallow. Granite from the Canadian Shield weathers very slowly, releases few important plant nutrients, and lacks the capacity to

moderate soil acidity. In such a rocky environment the majority of the soils are not ideally suited to agriculture, whereas both natural and managed forests can generally be quite productive in The Land Between.

Northern forests are, however, extremely susceptible to acid rain. This well-publicized phenomenon is one of the most pressing environmental issues in The Land Between. Positioned downwind from large industrial centres in Ohio and southwestern Ontario, and prone to precipitation, The Land Between receives regular doses of acidity. Because Shield soils lack calcium-rich minerals (such as those found in southern Ontario's sedimentary soils), the acid rain literally strips away whatever scarce nutrients may actually be present. These soils, increasingly acidified, in turn contribute to the process of allowing aluminium, a toxic element occurring naturally in many soils, to become "available" for plants, and often inadvertently taken up by them. In the 1980s and 1990s, reductions in sulphur emissions from industry made some headway in limiting acid rain. But in our atmosphere, rich in nitrogen and oxygen, combustion of nearly any type produces nitric acid as a by-product. Adding lime or nutrients to Shield soils has helped mitigate the effects of acid rain in the short term, but the problem will only wane as fossil fuel consumption decreases. This sensitive shallow shell of weathered minerals and decomposing plants both supports and constrains the great biodiversity for which The Land Between is known. Clearly soil is far more than simply dirt. ■

Rock outcrops—this one on Provincial Route 118 a few kilometres west of Carnarvon— clearly illustrate why tilling the soil in many parts of The Land Between has largely been futile. Yet the lush growth of sugar maple behind demonstrates that the site is far from barren. (photo courtesy of author)

4. Imagining The Land Between with Otto Jacobi

Brian S. Osborne

The "nature" of The Land Between has been rendered scientifically as an ecotone with its distinctive geology, topography and botany. It has been evaluated economically in terms of its settlement and resource potentials by surveyors, lumbermen, and prospectors. It has long been lived in as homeland by the First Nations, struggled with by potential settlers, and enjoyed by sojourning recreationists. The complex perception of this place is the result of all these encounters.

And there is another element that adds to this construction: imagination. Painters, poets, novelists, and sculptors have transformed the physicality of The Land Between into the ethereal world of artistic imagination. Otto Reinhold Jacobi—born in 1812 in Prussia, court painter to the Grand Duke of Nassau, landscape artist in the back of Frontenac County, president of the Royal Canadian Academy of Arts in 1890, and retired in North Dakota—became one of the first foreign-born artists to capture the uniqueness of the Canadian landscape.

In 1860, Jacobi settled in Montreal and was immediately commissioned to paint Shawinigan Falls as a gift to Edward, the young Prince of Wales then visiting from England. We may imagine that the strong German connection with the English monarchy, as well as the growing Romantic association many Germans made with wild places, rendered Jacobi the right man for the task. And connection with the Canadian wilderness only deepened as he moved into the Ottawa-Huron Tract north of Kingston. We read that Otto and his wife Sybille were ensconced in "our little wood cottage" on the shores of Malcolm Lake in 1876, near the new settlement of Ardoch in the back of Frontenac County. It was pioneer life with a touch of class: stories speak of two hefty Aboriginal canoes being commissioned to transport a rosewood square-grand piano across the lake to their retreat in the woods!

Nomination to the Ontario Society of Artists in 1877, and the constitution of the Royal Canadian Academy (RCA) three years later, centred Jacobi's future career in Toronto, although his cottage and garden on Malcolm Lake continued as did his connection with the wild rivers and forests he captured in his art. During the 1870s Jacobi had speculated in land, and through much of the 1880s he was dealing with debts while living variously in Philadelphia, Malcolm Lake, Montreal, and Toronto. Back once more to Toronto by 1890, he was President of the RCA for three years. With the death of Sybille in 1896, Jacobi emigrated to live with his daughter in Ardoch, North Dakota (after its Ontario namesake), where he died in 1901.

Otto Jacobi's odyssey is typical of so many immigrants in the second half of the nineteenth century, but few engaged with the land in the way he did. Registry records refer to farmers, shopkeepers, lumbermen, and stonemasons; few are "artists." And while those more

prosaic trades struggled to transform the forests of the Ottawa-Huron Tract into a settled and productive place, Jacobi pioneered in constructing Canadians' imagination of the rivers, hills, and mountains of the Shield as iconic statements of the land and their lived-experience of it.

To be sure, his *Emigrants Going West* (1865) is a highly romanticized allegory of the pioneer's experience with the wilderness, complete with a Native guide and sun setting in the west. It was an imaginative engagement with what he was to encounter realistically a decade later. Perhaps his *View on the Mississippi River—Ottawa Valley* (with Adolph Vogt) was not another idealized landscape but rather the product of a pre-location scouting of the region in which he was soon to settle. (And, yes, there is a Mississippi River, flowing off the eastern flank of The Land Between.) Stylized though a large number of his many landscape pieces may have been, others such as his *Clearing the Forest* (1872), *Sunrise* (1877) and *Sunset* (1877), *The Trapper's Cottage* (1878), and *Rapids* (1878) were prompted by his images and experience of The Land Between. ∎

Otto Jacobi and Adolph Vogt (1842-1871), another Montreal German painter, collaborated on "View on the Mississippi River—Ottawa Valley" (1866). (courtesy Musée du Québec)

5. Motoring the Three-Rut Road

Thomas F. McIlwraith

Ontario is known for its straight roads, and even sometimes in places where they ought not to be straight. Here, for instance, is the 13th Concession Road of Seymour Township, draped across The Land Between as it aims relentlessly through scrub forest towards Stanwood, a country crossroads hamlet that is situated where it is because surveyors running straight lines happened to cause two of their perpendiculars to intersect at that point. It is all so arbitrary.

Southward of Seymour, out across the benign farmlands of Hastings County, straight road allowances and squared-off farm boundaries took hold with ease, only occasionally deferring to the slightly rumpled topography. Northward towards Algonquin Park the surveyor's grid has been all but ignored. In The Land Between occurs the stand-off between disdain and submission. Here, along the 13th of Seymour, the uncompromising survey system seems to have trumped ecology. Steep swooping grades at one moment offer vistas and the urge to "floor it," yet give way, a moment later, to a blind hill and the thrill of surprise at what may lie just over the crest. Linearity has its price.

The 13th of Seymour is one of many roads in The Land Between that is loose-surfaced. Is a hard asphalt strip about to be rolled out on this right-of-way, or is it forever to remain a gravel road? Which way, technologically-speaking, is the 13th of Seymour going? One cannot paint a central stripe on gravel, and a hard paintable surface would have to be appreciably wider, to

provide full-width lanes in each direction, leading to the faster motoring that hard surfaces invariably produce. Here in Seymour, the roads department has saved on paint, asphalt and roadbed by leaving many kilometres as loose gravel.

Seymour has come up with, or perhaps lucked into, a clever solution: the three-rut road. The smooth tan-coloured tire lanes are separated by almost perfect gravel windrows. Drivers in both directions aim along the middle rut, and the right-side wheels occupy the marginal ones. That's just enough hedging against someone coming in the opposite direction, yet the manicured windrows tell me that a "meet" seldom occurs. The three-rut road is a democratic solution, generated by sensible users in a district where traffic—more than one vehicle at a time—is to all intents and purposes unknown, where roads appear to be too big for their needs.

The 13th of Seymour well may be a racetrack for youth on a Saturday night, but the three ruts adroitly discourage the road hog

from careering menacingly down the middle. Leave that sort of behaviour to the lower status side road that connects the 13th with concession lines parallel to it. Nearby, the side-road between lots eighteen and nineteen in Concession fourteen of Seymour is just such a road, showing only two ruts and no shoulder at all. For two vehicles to arrive here head-on at the same instant must be highly unlikely. The alternation of rut and windrow in the two-rut road is the reverse from those on the three-rut version. This is truly a one-way (either way) road—down the middle. Ecology is squeezing in on the survey, and now a small outcrop of rock or a beaver pond is enough to shake the road from its appointed path. Some will even run out, the subtle gravel strip down the centre evolving into a bold swath of grass of impending finality.

From paved highway to boggy footpath, the successive decline of the public road is a powerful expression of the heightened diversity of phenomena in the transitional landscape, The Land Between. ∎

6. The Land Between Imagined

Rae B. Fleming

When I was growing up in the southerly part of The Land Between, I used to hear stories about people who were born in, who moved to, or who explored this ribbon of land that swings southeast from Georgian Bay to the Rideau and Frontenac areas of Ontario. In fact, it is these stories, spawned by The Land Between and sticking in my head all these years that, for me at least, have created its identity.

My childhood home was the village of Argyle, not far south of the Trent Canal and the adjacent Portage Road, which together are the most historic transportation routes in The Land Between. Family members told me of Samuel de Champlain and his Huron guides, arduously portaging their canoes the many miles between Lake Simcoe and Balsam Lake almost three centuries before the Kirkfield Lift Lock was opened in 1907. Had I doubted this story, a trip to Champlain's monument in Orillia would affirm that he had indeed passed through The Land Between, in 1615. At the corner of the Portage Road and Highway 46, a few minutes north of Argyle, Champlain passed the future site of Biddy Young's Tavern. A century and more ago Biddy distilled her

Jean Munro, originally from Orillia, depicts in soft tones what is nevertheless a miserly landscape, characteristic of so much of The Land Between encountered by settlers early in the 20th century. (author's collection)

own whiskey, acted as her own bouncer, and sauced judges who lectured her on home brewing. Old-timers still speak of Biddy Young's Corner.

My grandfather used to tell his children about Sir William Mackenzie, born in Kirkfield in 1849. "How did he get his title, and how did he make so much money?" I used to ask. No one knew. I couldn't ask Grandfather Mitchell, for he had died five months before my birth. Overwhelmed by curiosity,

I wrote a biography of Mackenzie, and then I knew: railways, the surest path to fortune (or, for some less savvy, disaster) in Victorian Canada.

Another notable Land Betweener was Leslie Frost, born in Orillia in 1895 and Premier of Ontario from 1949 to 1961. When I was about eight years old, I caught a glimpse of Premier Frost, though I had to ask the identity of the tall, silver-haired man emerging from Woodville United Church, surrounded by a crowd of deferential locals dressed uncomfortably in their Sunday best. Frost had just attended the funeral of William Newman—"Buttermilk Bill"—his old Liberal rival who, in 1934, had defeated the novice Conservative candidate, Leslie Frost, in the provincial election. Bill was co-owner of a creamery in Lorneville, and some of his butter came from the scatter of domestic dairy cows raised on the beef cattle lands north of the Trent Canal—a typical mixed livestock style in The Land Between.

My part of The Land Between has been imagined by writers such as Stephen Leacock, who invented Mariposa, a thinly-veiled parody of Orillia, near where he spent many summers. Then there was Dennis T. Patrick Sears, who grew up near the old Victoria Colonization Road, built to encourage newcomers to settle on the barely-camouflaged limestone rock of The Land Between. Sears set his *Lark in the Clear Air* in the fictionalized village of Victoria Road. My father's cousin Ernie thought the book was rather tame, at least as compared to his own memories of bootleggers, wily cattle buyers who wore spats (one was a retired professor of Latin and Greek), and not-so-secret trysts on Fanny Hill. And not far south of Victoria Road lived the Laidlaws, more characters straight out of fiction. There was George the father, indefatigable railroad fund-raiser of the 1870s known by the moniker "the prince of bonus hunters." One son, Colonel George, rode across western Canada wearing chaps that still hang in his old cottage on Balsam Lake. Another son, "one-armed Jim," once tried to cheat farmers on the weight of cattle, an indiscretion that, for one day at least, drew together English Methodists and Irish Catholics in expelling him from the Victoria Road cattle pen. Laidlaws remain to this day rather proud of their ancestry.

To this entourage add the artist Jean Cockburn Munro. Born in Orillia in 1868, she was the daughter of A. P. Cockburn, once reeve of Kirkfield and the founder of steamboating in the Muskokas. Jean was an artist who, I imagine, carried The Land Between with her throughout her life—to California, Paris, Venice, North Africa, Brittany, Normandy and, finally, Montreal and Toronto. Though mostly forgotten today, in 1921 Munro was awarded honorary mention by the Société des artistes français, perhaps for *Vimy Qui Renait*. She opened a studio in Westmount in 1926. Her love of the Laurentians is manifested in what may be her masterpiece, *Village in the Laurentians*. I used to visit Jean Munro's cousin Mary Fowler, in Beaverton, custodian of eight Munro oils. How I admired those paintings—visual support for my lifetime of The Land Between stories—and when Mary died in the mid-1990s, I purchased the lot. This one—rudimentary building, rail fence, rough fields and stone outcrop—I like to believe depicts The Land Between. Yes, it is rather bluer than Ontario, perhaps a carry-over from Munro's years in France; as with most of her pieces, it is untitled. It is certainly Canadian, and could be the Gatineau Hills, but I prefer to think that it is Haliburton a century ago, or perhaps old Muskoka, where one of Jean's father's steamboats, the restored *Seguin*, still plies the waters of The Land Between. ∎

7. Thinking about the White Oak

Rory Eckenswiller

A mature white oak (*Quercus alba*) is a huge and truly majestic tree, rising as much as 35 metres—the height of a ten-storey building—and up to 120 cm in diameter. White oaks are known to live for hundreds of years, and in The Land Between they are indeed elegant showpieces. The round-lobed leaves, hand-sized or bigger, distinguish it from other oaks. The pale grey bark often has a reddish cast and is scaly, and the acorn fruit is broadly bowl-shaped. The wood is strong and very hard, and commonly light brown in colour. The trees are moderately tolerant to shade and can grow in a variety of soil textures and depths.

The white oak is at its northern limit in The Land Between. It does not simply fade away, however, but strikes a robust presence in many varieties of broadleaved forests. Its occurrence with white birch, which is at the southern limit of its range, is a subtle but significant signal that woodland containing both oak and birch is distinctive, perhaps even unique, to The Land Between. And white oak may be found not only in forests, but also in the scrubby regenerated fields scattered throughout The Land Between, sometimes along old fence lines and on other occasions standing in solitary splendour in the open, where once cattle gathered for shade on hot summer afternoons. Special clusters are found in savannas near Minden, and near Kingston, in combination with such species as Canada blue grass (*Poa compressa*) and poverty grass (*Panicum acamination*). Being called "white oak savannas" is a clear indication of the trees' importance in these limestone plains of shallow soils so characteristic of The Land Between.

There is no doubt that the white oak of The Land Between is a hardy tree, and one wonders if it has developed special survival strategies. In the central part of The Land Between white oak grows in generally sub-optimal soil conditions, with (alkaline) limestone dominant; such settings are quite unlike the deep rich soils on which the tree flourishes further south. To the east, the white oak may be different again, here frequently avoiding limestone soils. Perhaps it is related to oak in the Ottawa valley and southern Quebec. Altogether, there is good reason to imagine that there are a number of subspecies of white oak, each adapted in a slightly different manner to local conditions. This variation would make a worthy research, and it certainly underscores the biodiversity for which The Land Between is known.

Botanists have wondered why the white oak, so

close to the limit of its range, exists in The Land Between at all. Has it migrated from elsewhere? Are the little oak islands relict communities left over from an era of warmer temperatures thousands of years ago? Have First Nations communities protected oak, knowing that their acorns attracted game for hunting? Has the preference of the eastern grey squirrel for red oak acorns (which are more durable than white oak acorns) inhibited the spreading of white oak? Before readers contemplate a squirrel conspiracy, it is worth noting that zoologists have published treatises on squirrels' acorn preferences and their shortcomings as distributors of white oak acorns into new territory.

A great deal of thinking remains speculative, however, and correlations and connections among facts are yet to be worked out. Numerous questions invite thoughtful study. Mike McMurty, ecologist, and Don Southerland, zoologist, of the National Heritage Information Centre in Peterborough have started into the daunting task of collecting evidence from throughout the region with which to move forward from speculation to understanding. A massive cooperative venture is required, recording information and feeding it to a centralized database. Here is one simple instance in which individual citizens may contribute to the wider understanding of The Land Between as a special ecotone. I have no doubt Peter Alley would have been an eager participant. ∎

8. "The Chemical" at Donald

John Wadland

On County Road 1, just south of the village of Haliburton, stands the hamlet of Donald, named for R. A. Donald of Markham, Ontario, who in 1906 recognized the potential of area hardwoods to supply fuel for the charcoal iron industry. Beyond the bed of the old Victoria Railway (now a recreational trail), through the trees, rears the skeleton of Mr. Donald's dream—the Canada Wood Products Company plant.

"The Chemical" was a monstrous aberration in the wilderness, and described in a pre-World War I newspaper article as being "built entirely of brick and reinforced concrete, where hundreds of tons of steel lie hidden in vast walls, floors and towers of cement [and] crushed limestone brought from the [local] Somerville quarry. Here are placed immense engines, steam and power pumps, gas generators, huge condensers and ovens large enough to receive several cords of wood at a time, above which rise vast smokestacks designed to belch clouds of smoke toward the skies." Such prose calls to mind the "dark satanic mills" in that "green and pleasant land" of Hubert Parry's stirring hymn, "Jerusalem."

This rural monument is neither beautiful nor architecturally distinctive; it is a remnant of an industrial landscape created to feed "progress." In the 19th and early 20th centuries foundries relied upon charcoal for smelting malleable and chilled pieces of iron into intricate, stress-resistant shapes that were light and inexpensive. These products were especially desired by railways and farm implement manufacturers. In Haliburton, hardwood for the produc-

CHEMICAL WORKS, DONALD, NEAR HALIBURTON, ONT.

The recipient of this smudged postcard, dated about 1920, learns that the Canada Wood Products Company Plant near Haliburton stands ringed by hardwood forest, waiting to be cut, stacked, steamed and sent out as charcoal to smelters in southern Ontario. In the 21st century that forest is reclaiming its ground, smothering remnants of "The Chemical." (private collection)

tion of charcoal was plentiful and cheap. Up to 50 cords a day—more than 15,000 cords a year—were fed into Donald's sealed, airtight ovens, heated to 900 degrees Celsius for twenty-four hours, cooled, and then packed onto trains for southern Ontario foundries. With three shifts, the plant operated round the clock, six days a week.

Following World War I, by-products distilled from the gases given off by the charring process became more valued than the charcoal. But acetate of lime (used to make weapons-grade explosives) and methyl alcohol (for cleaning solvents and anti-freeze) could not sustain an obsolete, remote installation, and the plant closed in 1946. Petrochemical technology had antiquated the Donald plant. As "The Chemical" settles back into the ground, the ghosts of its 300-man workforce are recalled in the stories of the remaining community.

The Donald site was attractive because of its proximity to the rail line, opened nearly thirty years before R. A. came on the scene. The plant transformed the economy of Haliburton County, creating secure, waged jobs, and introducing quantities of recent Italian and Finnish immigrants to augment the labour force in cutting, in concentric circles beyond the plant, virtually every living hard maple tree in the bioregion. The company owned and operated the store, post office, and community centre; it built and

rented rooms in a boarding house and detached homes to which it supplied electricity and hot water from the steam generator in the factory. The generator and cooling ovens drew their water from the nearby Burnt River. Hauling wood was originally a job for teamsters, conducted only in winter over snow and ice roads. Horses were replaced by a huge Lynn caterpillar tractor in 1922, and ultimately by trucks, which encouraged road building and year-round cutting still farther afield. The more sophisticated the technology, the more rapid the depletion of the hardwood forest.

Southern Ontario industry depended then, as today, upon hinterland plants which exploited immigrant and Aboriginal workers and laid waste the surrounding environment. Now, in the 21st century, a plan is being implemented to stabilize the ruins of "The Chemical." By preserving them for the children of the Haliburton bioregion and The Land Between, Donald takes on the role of a metaphor for Canada and for the place those youngsters occupy in its history. This remnant landscape—their heritage—is explained in part by complex chemical processes which required the consumption of a forest in the production of weapons to make the world safe for democracy. Donald is a history lesson, a chemistry lesson, an economics lesson, and an ecology lesson all rolled into one. ∎

9. The Natural Night

Robert Dick

In the 1920s my grandfather purchased our family property on Rideau Lake, at the eastern limit of The Land Between. There, in the 1960s, I watched the stars reflect off the still water, and fell asleep to the call of the loons and the chorus of frogs, crickets, and beetles. By the 1970s, however, this idyll had begun to change. Rideau Lake was evolving into an urban subdivision

The Milky Way hovers above The Land Between in late summer. (photo courtesy of author)

with fast boats, outdoor sound systems and—particularly disturbing—shore lighting that remained on throughout the night. The faint starlight was being overwhelmed by the glare of electric lights, a symbol of our affluent, self-serving society, and promoted by cheap electricity—"live better electrically"—and the erroneous belief that light is benign and makes the world safe.

Much of The Land Between missed out on the modernization that has lit up Rideau Lake and urban Canada generally. This circumstance has preserved for the residents the darker places to contemplate, and come to appreciate the night sky. All life on Earth has evolved with the need for bright days and dark nights. Nocturnal animals take advantage of the anonymity provided by darkness to elude predators as they forage for food using the stars to navigate across the landscape. If you stand quietly in an open field on a summer night—you are not alone. The land teems with wildlife. To me the sounds of nature provide a fitting ambiance to the visual spectacle above my head. But even the light of the full Moon for a week or so each month forces nocturnal animals to change their foraging behaviour. Fortunately for these vocal nocturnal creatures, three weeks of relative darkness follow, whereas the urban sky glow is never truly dark.

The celestial sphere is a world of its own. The constellations are like celestial nations and the stars are like teaming towns and cities. Standing under a clear dark sky exposes one to a vista that has hardly changed in millions of years. The glowing band of the Milky Way dominates the late-summer sky as it crosses from the northeast in the constellations of Perseus and Cassiopeia, overhead through Cygnus the swan and Aquila the eagle, and down to the southwest with Sagittarius and Scorpius and the bright centre of our galaxy. The Milky Way is mottled with dark clouds of interstellar dust and embellished with concentrated star fields. Scanning the skies with only binoculars in hand, we cruise through bright glowing nebulae in which stars are formed, and distant star fields drift in and out of view along with dark dust clouds that block the light of more distant suns. Take time, barely ten minutes, to let our eyes adapt to the darkness, so we can more fully appreciate what the night sky offers. And do not miss the Milky Way in winter, though weakened to a subtle glow punctuated by bright nearby stars of our own galactic spiral arm. For all the grandeur of Orion the hunter, winter is a time of frigid solitude. The sounds of nature are silent but for the cracking of sap in the frozen trees and the snap and boom of ice flexing and shifting on the snowy lake.

The economic uncertainty that persisted in The Land Between through so much of the 20th century has provided a hiatus during which society has come to appreciate the importance of a balanced environment and the perils implicit in changing it. Yet few people have placed light pollution in the same category of environmental damage as water or air pollution, or even paused to think about it. As we enter the 21st century, the darkest and most accessible skies in Ontario flow across The Land Between, hanging there waiting for a society gradually awakening to the richness of this simplest of treasures.

My grandfather would be pleased. ■

10. A Limestone Island in a Granite Sea

Alan G. Brunger

On Highway 36, between Buckhorn and Burleigh Falls, stands a modest concrete block residence which once served as a community centre and, before 1968, as a one-room school. This 1930s building marks the erstwhile community of Deer Bay, and replaces the original frame schoolhouse erected in 1898. This historical sequence is a testament to the vibrant community that persisted for several generations on a flat-topped hill near the southern border of The Land Between. In the local vernacular such a hill is known as a ledge (or sometimes a flat), in recognition of its almost horizontal layers of limestone which rise up abruptly from the generally rugged surface of the Canadian Shield.

Like islands in a sea of granite, the limestone ledges of The Land Between welcomed to their shores a surge of optimistic settlers about the time

45

of Canadian Confederation. The Deer Bay ledge was one of those lime-stone havens. And when, almost a century later, the tide of abandonment ebbed across much of the area, Deer Bay continued to stand out, high and dry, a refuge for a persisting farming community.

The geological story of the ledge is rooted in the ancient granites of the Canadian Shield, worn down over hundreds of millions of years of river and glacial erosion. Atop this base the rocks forming Deer Bay and countless other hills subsequently accumulated as coral and the remains of a multitude of organisms under a tropical ocean. These sediments gradually turned to limestone, became interbedded with sand, silt and clay, and hardened into level, horizontal layers which slowly rose above sea level, slightly tilted. They eventually formed dry land which was in turn worn away, mainly by rivers, revealing in some places the underlying Canadian Shield.

This process of erosion proceeded generally from north to south, the residual edge forming a low, sinuous ridge with irregularities caused by random variations in the hardness and structure of the sedimentary rock. Northward-projecting peninsulas overlooked the Shield in some places; else-where the sediments were worn back far to the south. Some of the peninsulas became entirely cut off from the ridge, becoming offshore, flat-topped, mesa-like islands with steep sides: the ledges of The Land Between. The remains of the community of Deer Bay stands on one of these ledge islands.

The light grey tones of the limestone ledges of Deer Bay, and else-where, signify their coral, lime-rich origin. These hues contrast with the reddish-brown granites and generally darker-coloured metamorphic rocks of the surrounding Shield. The soils of the ledges are slightly deeper and more fertile than those of the Shield and were thus able to sustain some farming—both crop cultivation and grazing. However, by the late 20th century the changing economy of The Land Between had left few farms, even on the ledges, and almost all that persist are part-time operations. But the evidence of agricultural communities on the ledges survives, visible in the farmhouses, outbuildings, cedar-rail fences, piles of stones cleared from former fields, scattered country churches and, of course, rural schools such as the one at Deer Bay. ■

The school at Deer Bay, near the edge of the ledge.

11. The Land Between at the Frontenac Arch

Brian S. Osborne

Where is this image (page 50)? It shows the junction of the Palaeozoic limestone with the Precambrian Shield. It even has the transition from the mixed deciduous forest to the coniferous as evidenced by the solitary pine to the right! Is it Severn Bridge, Madoc or Kaladar? Perhaps near Loughborough Lake or Seeley's Bay?

No. None of the above. It's on Highway 401 at the junction with Highway 15, just east of Kingston and within sight of the St. Lawrence River, overlooking the Thousand Islands. The Land Between ecotone, properly identified by Peter Alley, continue southeastward into the Frontenac Arch of the Canadian Shield, known to some as "A2A"—the corridor running from Algonquin Park to the Adirondacks in New York State. In 2002, the Thousand Islands-Frontenac Arch section of A2A was recognized by UNESCO as a World Heritage Bioreserve. Ecological uniqueness aside, it too is associated with material expressions and memories of The Land Between: the First Nations' presence, pioneer settlement experiences, and shifting economic and aesthetic priorities.

It was in this region that the Iroquois forayed out from the French base at Fort Frontenac in their pursuit of beaver. And here, following the arrival of British military and Loyalist settlers in 1783, the new occupiers of the land, the Mississauga, gradually ceded lands, including some three million acres (about 1.2 million hectares) of the Ottawa-Huron Tract—The Land Between!—in 1819-22. Surrender No. 77 of 1856 terminated the Mississauga claim to all the islands in the Upper St. Lawrence as far down stream as Prescott.

The end of the formal Native presence in the Thousand Islands was also, ironically, the beginning of remembering. At the same time as the First Nations were being physically displaced and socially marginalized, a burgeoning tourism industry appropriated their former presence and rendered their story in place names and romantic tropes. These have entered the national imagination, ensuring their continued presence in The Land Between.

There was little, however, to prompt a romanticizing of farm settlement in the knobs and swamps of The Land Between back of Kingston. A tantalizing scatter of glacial clays

and sands and beaver meadows enticed the optimistic settlers, but there were always realists who reminded potential farmers of the essential problem. In 1792, Alex Aitken, who had been contracted to survey Pittsburgh Township along the St. Lawrence, abandoned his task by asserting that "I would be putting Government to a useless expense to Survey lands that will never be settled." Twenty years later the social commentator Robert Gourlay observed that "Kingston is subject to one local disadvantage, the want of a populous back country." By the 1840s, objectors to Kingston's claim to being the Provincial capital complained that the "country around is unproductive."

But there were always the boosters. The Midland District Land Company was formed in 1835 to stimulate Kingston's back country. It urged immigrants to go beyond the "gloomy woods" of Portland and encounter the "fine lands" of Hinchinbrook, Olden, and parts of Loughborough "with their small crystal lakes of countless numbers, their rivers and rivulets, and springs, not of muddy and stagnant waters … and all abounding with fish." As if this was not enough, "[the] very sight of the timber itself … is sufficient to convince any judge of the fertility of the soil." Hundreds of families heeded the call and strove to turn wilderness into fields and forests into potash and lumber, but not without trials and tribulations! We read of "a hopeless country" and the plough scraping the Shield over desperately thin soil. Fortunately,

the Frontenac Arch section of The Land Between afforded another opportunity: minerals. Limited agricultural returns could be supplemented by the many scattered deposits of mica, phosphate, lead, zinc, and iron, anticipating larger deposits farther north in The Land Between.

By the mid-19th century, a new focus on wild places as sites of restoration and communion with nature was emerging. Contemporary developments—the Rideau Canal, steamships, and railways—connected burgeoning cities in Canada and the United States with the Frontenac Arch and The Land Between as a whole. Entrepreneurs built hotels to accommodate sports fishers and upper-class vacationers. As elsewhere in The Land Between, seasonal homes and mass tourism followed, attracted by the spiritual, sublime, and picturesque elements of this distinctive area.

Looking down from Fort Henry Heights southward onto Cedar Island, I gaze over the place where Lake Ontario becomes the St. Lawrence River. But it is also where the grey strata of Palaeozoic limestone—fabric for the two Martello towers visible—overlie the granite of the Canadian Shield. Here, at Cedar Island, we find the easterly face of The Land Between. To the south it continues to the Adirondacks; to the north it extends across Ontario to Algonquin. And between these two poles of the A2A, The Land Between exists both as a scientific ecotone and as a distinctive human experience. ∎

12. A Cool Curving World: An Excerpt

*Richard B. Miller**

Georgian Bay is in my blood. Literally. When we paddle out to the Open, I drink that sweet water right out of my hand. As a sixth-generation cottager, my childhood memories are shared by many others who spent summers barefoot on hot rock, scented with white pine, the sound of waves lapping us into sleep. My great-uncle, Birnie Hodgetts, founded Camp Huron-tario (as described by Claire Campbell in this volume), and Richard B. Miller, my paternal grandmother's first cousin, wrote the following account of his summers at the Bay. His stories, and many like them, have been passed down in our family and among the old-timers of Cognashene. Despite the changes to the landscape—both created and observed by each generation—this memoir speaks to the eternal elements of water, wind, and rock in our beloved Georgian Bay.

—Rebecca Pollock

The curving world of Georgian Bay. (photo courtesy of David S. Bywater)

* Excerpted from Richard B. Miller. A Cool Curving World. Winnipeg: Longmans, 1962. 63-68. Miller would have first been to the Georgian Bay as a baby in 1915 and probably spent all or part of every summer there until one year of age. These thoughts were probably first conceived during a visit to the family cottage in 1944.

"…I am the third generation of the family to spend summers there; I have spent at least a part of nearly every summer of my life on the [Georgian] Bay, beginning when I was three months old. Our part is the Thirty Thousand Islands region—the loveliest vacation land that I have ever seen, provided you like vacations which do not include golf and dancing…

In spite of the solid, immutable stone, the Bay is as flexible and pliant as a woman. There are the gay, laughing, bright days, with a gentle northwest wind and a sky as blue as a prairie sky; the water dances and sparkles in the light, the aspens chuckle in the swamps and the pines on the headlands sway and roll in merry rhythm. On such days it is pure joy to spank along in a small sailboat, untroubled by noise of engines or smells of exhaust fumes. Or one can sit on the camp veranda, and gaze out beyond the fringing reefs to the open, where sky and water meet, and the distant grain freighters reveal their routes by long trails of dark smoke rising above the water's curved edge.

Then there are the sultry days, common in August, when all is still and the heat haze shimmers on the horizon. The inside passage is a sheet of molten metal on which the islands float, and every tree and rock is repeated, upside down, below them. At these times one sits in the water, or pants on the veranda, remarking at frequent intervals how awful it must be in the cities…

When my grandparents first came to the islands there were almost no cottages and very few campers. A large tent, like a side-show tent, but pitched on a wooden floor, is my earliest recollection of our camp. Inside it was divided into bedrooms by canvas strung on wires. Occupying the bedrooms were four of us children, my parents, my aunt and uncle, and my maternal grandmother. A small shack with a coal-oil stove was the kitchen, and our dining room was the great out-of-doors. A long dining table with built-on benches stood on a pine-needle carpet under the trees….

Nowadays there is no substitute for some of the early camping pleasures. Going to the supply boat was one of the greatest of these. We all piled into my grandmother's big, broad eighteen-foot canoe, taking the coal-oil can and grocery baskets, and cushions to sit on. We paddled round our point and down into the next deep passage, where there was a cottage with a proper dock and enough water. Here the supply boat tied up for a few hours and waited for the visits of the campers of the area. These arrived in gay parties like ours, in canoes and rowboats. Motor boats were not too common. The supply boat itself was a trim little black-and-white excursion steamer, the *City of Dover*, converted into a floating grocery store. The novelty of shopping on a boat, the surety of candy and pop, the hustle and bustle and comings and goings, made this a gala event for the kids.

I still enjoy visiting the Bay; for one thing, my parents are there. But much of its early charm has been lost. Almost every island has a cottage; some cottages are built on islands so small that kitchens or porches project out over the water. The inside passage is alive with boats— trim launches, angry little outboards, and beautiful white private yachts. Hydro-electric power poles step from island to island, carrying their ugly wires. The great saving grace is the scattered nature of the islands; it renders impossible the crowding of cottages into regular tight rows which so ruins the appeal of most popular summer resorts. So the feeling of spaciousness and freedom persists…." ∎

13. Cottaging: A Life of Liminality

Nik Luka

Waterfront "cottage" landscapes are hard to dissociate from The Land Between in popular imagination, and with good reason. Attempts to colonize Ontario's Near North for agriculture in the 19th century met with little success, and logging was short-lived. It was tourism and outdoor leisure pursuits that eventually became mainstays. Back in the Victorian era tourism involved summer resorts, but these have largely given way

The Land Between signals the transition many Ontarians experience as they move between being city-dwellers and cottagers. (photo collage courtesy of author)

Stoney Lake

to the cottage—a private second home—and these have proliferated in the later 20th century. As towns in the older parts of southern Ontario grew into industrial cities in the 19th century, people of means began to go elsewhere for the summer, seeking more healthful settings offering rich out-of-doors experiences and symbolic meaning. The landscapes of second homes within The Land Between—"cottage country"—have since come to be associated with wealth, power, success, and other qualities that drive so much of human behaviour. These waterfront settings offer expressions of Canadian folklore: the pioneer spirit, life in the forested north country, and a sense of connection with nature. Here are the spaces for play and sites for swimming and boating.

Viewed northward from the Lake Ontario front, The Land Between has acted as a threshold for cottaging. It marks a climatic transition, being the southerly limit of fresh westerly winds bringing cooler, unpolluted "non-city" air. Here, too, the gently rolling St. Lawrence Lowlands yield to the craggy, lake-dappled Shield, where people do "non-city" things. The sparseness of settlement, together with the sorts of work people can do with the land, adds a cultural component that contrasts sharply with the metropolis. It all offers a natural richness that people have come to value. The Land Between is a threshold that most people can sense and readily recognize, if only subconsciously.

The Land Between may be seen as a set of landscapes which most cottage folk merely traverse. The Land Between is distinguished by its liminality—literally, the condition of becoming something else. One may identify as "liminal" particular changes that are once-and-for-all, such as the rite of passage from adolescence into adulthood. However, architects, land planners, and social anthropologists also use the term to describe spaces or "moments" marking a transition that is repeated time and again, often in a ritualistic way, tying the two parts together like a bridge. Doorways, front porches, bridges, and even urban waterfronts are liminal, thresholds that are important not just for passing across but also as spaces in which one wishes to linger, where special qualities can be experienced. Families with cottages find great meaning in the act of "dwelling through multiple places." In the city or suburb they find opportunities for work, education, and access to services, whereas in their cottage setting they embrace other qualities: opportunities for play, relaxing rules and schedules, and having fun fixing up the "extra" dwelling. Switching between city and cottage seems to help make life more enjoyable, and in this way the liminal moments of travelling back and forth are important. Each year several hundred thousand cottagers visit, appropriate, or traverse the landscapes of The Land Between in an everyday manner.

The Land Between has long been an ecotone of biodiversity within which cottaging has added a layer of cultural diversity that significantly adds to its complexity. Thresholds across and through it are countless in number. Is The Land Between destined to remain a zone one traverses between the cityscapes to the south and the rugged woodlands to the north? Is being liminal what The Land Between will forever be about? We may be obliged to answer this question sooner rather than later, in order to develop sustainable ways to relieve population pressures in the Greater Toronto Area. Will cottaging visitors pause, and perhaps settle? Will they immerse themselves in The Land Between, and, by so doing, will they establish new thresholds reflecting Ontario's increasingly multicultural reality? Liminality has so many dimensions. Time will tell. ∎

14. Memoir from Curve Lake First Nation

Murray Whetung

Curve Lake Reserve was surveyed and divided into two types of lots. There were village lots which were about four to eight acres, and what Indian Affairs called farm lots, which were about forty to fifty acres. My father had a village lot and a farm lot. He had a barn on the village lot and a house. He kept a team of horses, some cows and pigs in the barn at the village lot where he also had a general store. The farm lot would not grow anything but rocks and trees.

When my father was getting ready to retire he asked me if I wanted the store or the wooded farm lot. I took the wooded lot because I thought I would just let the store run down; I am good-natured and would give everything away to friends and neighbours.

My father was sent to Residential School when he was a boy. He didn't talk about it except that he said the

A barrier of birch trees warns us to be cautious when venturing out onto the lake in winter.
(photograph courtesy of Leora Berman)

only thing he learnt there was to drive a team of horses. He always had to have horses. We had two horses, a rough-like young gelding and an old skinny mare. The horses were kept to do work like ploughing gardens, cutting hay for the cows, drawing wood home for the fires that heated the houses and also for cooking, and sometimes, when it was really cold in the winter we could either tow the car around with the horses until it would start or use the horses for transportation.

One time when I was about four or five years' young my father and mother, two brothers and a schoolteacher, whose name was Art Smith, and I went to Buckhorn to visit my mother's parents. That afternoon we were coming home from there by sleigh down the lake. My father was driving the team of horses along the same track we had used in the morning going over to Buckhorn.

About halfway down the lake suddenly there was a crunching splashing sound and the horses were swimming in broken ice and water. My father jumped off the sleigh and unhooked the harness from the sleigh, then went to the front of the horses and separated them. Then one horse jumped up onto the ice. My father then told my oldest brother to ride that horse home as fast as he would go, put him in the stable and put a horse blanket on him. Then go up to the house and start the fire in the cook stove and put two or three pots of water on to heat.

Then he began to try and get the other horse out of the hole in the ice. He was not having any success, so I'm standing up on the sleigh and yelling at him to take that horse over to the side where the first one had gotten out. He yelled back at me to leave him alone because what do you know about getting horses back up on the ice when they have broken through. Just then one of his legs went through the ice and left him sitting down. Before he could get up, the horse that was swimming went over to the other side of the hole where the first horse got out and jumped up on the ice.

He then got up and told my brother Clifford to get on that horse and ride it fast home to the stable and put her in the stall, take off the harness and put a horse blanket on her, then go up to the house and see if the water was warm and if it was get two pails and take it down and give each horse a pail of warm water to drink.

The rest of us walked home after that. ■

15. Remembering Camp Hurontario

Claire Elizabeth Campbell

In my father's favourite photograph of me, I am wearing a snake.

I'm about four years old, standing in front of the biology building at Camp Hurontario. I'm wearing the kind of tacky striped shirt that everybody seemed to wear in the 1970s, but you tend not to notice that, because hanging around my neck is a fox snake that is at least as long as I am tall.

There is a generational symmetry to this story, for my father was roughly the same age when my family first became entwined with the camp and the Georgian Bay. In 1950, my widowed grandmother was working as a secretary at Trinity College School, a boys' boarding school in Port Hope. A teacher by the name of Birnie Hodgetts had started a camp in the Thirty Thousand Islands, north of Twelve Mile Bay, and asked my grandmother to manage the office work. She agreed, and brought my six-year-old father to the camp island for the first time that summer.

The archipelago forms a ragged western border to The Land Between — a littoral between the rough waters of an inland sea and the sturdy forests of the old Ottawa-Huron Tract. Even in 1950 most of the islands still seemed remote and wild, accessible only by boat and preferred by those who

styled themselves as "woodsy." My father would spend thirty years at Hurontario, as camper, coun

60

sellor, and assistant director, bringing my (reluctant) mother in 1973, an infant daughter in 1974, and my brother two years later. The camp, he said once, was the great love of his life. The imprint of the Bay on his children would be fainter, for we spent less time there, but no less indelible.

My memories of the camp are tactile, sensual, but fragmented. Trying to hold a painted turtle at the terrarium, its webbed feet brushing unhappily against my hands. Climbing onto a porch to peer into the tiny cabin my grandmother called an office. Watching my father and other counsellors play "mud ball" in the charitably-named Sandy Bay on the back of the camp island. The smell of sun-warmed pine needles drying in rock crevices, of gasoline from the Boat House, of creosote on the docks.

Landscape critic Jay Appleton argues that our definition of beauty reflects primal, innate survival instincts: we are drawn to landscapes that afford us either the ability to see surrounding dangers (the prospect) or to hide from them (the refuge). When I first read this—while writing a dissertation on the Georgian Bay, twenty years after my snake-wearing days—I was struck by how true it seemed, how well it explained my attachment to a place I rarely saw.

First, the prospect: from an outer island, with a clear view to the Open, my father would point out distant landmarks like O'Donnell's Point or the Christian Islands. There is the exhilaration of space, the freedom to run along bare, tilting bedrock, pausing to nervously reach my toe across a gaping crevice. Buffeted by the full force of the wind, only patches of lichen and moss take hold here, with basalt, quartz, and rose granite sparkling in a spectrum of muted colour.

But a few steps back from the shoreline, and here is the refuge. Knee-high juniper spreading across the rock, then a sheltering confusion of paths across the camp island, between moss-covered boulders and rough-skinned oak. Here the crash of waves is muted to a dull, constant roar, overladen by the sound of wind in the taller pines. The geography is absorbed unconsciously, following a parent, stepping carefully around exposed tree roots. When I returned as an adult I somehow knew the way past old, dark, wooden cabins to Smiling Pool (so childish a name! Were the 40s really so innocent?). Lemon and white water lilies are frustratingly, securely rooted, while delicate cardinal flowers cluster along the shore.

The pairing of exposure and seclusion, of energy and tranquility, suggests what poet A.J.M. Smith called "a beauty of dissonance." My memories of the camp are tinted by nostalgia, by my father's love for the place. But it is as part of me as surely as any place on this Earth.

A few acres of pines and cedars where he knew
almost every tree. Abrupt granite rising from the clearest
water in all the world. Crowned with a tangled diadem
of blue green foliage...
And always beneath birdsong the sound of water.
Tonight he is imagining the calm after a three-day blow,
the roar of the open from the swell on the outer reefs,
while here on the inner islands the waves are gently lapping...

Douglas LePan,
"Islands of Summer," 1987 ∎

16. Hiding One's Age

Thomas F. McIlwraith

The Buick proclaimed its age—1957—in digits, right there on the hood ornament for all to see. That was a fine pronouncement in 1956, but had become a liability by 1958, and the idea was seldom, if ever, repeated. In so many ways we try hard to cover our tracks, and here, in The Land Between, it's no different. Someone has gone to painstaking length to remove the date from the manufacturer's identification plate on a handsome little truss bridge near Havelock.

Questions spring to mind. Was "1912" removed because the Wight's Island bridge was not put up in 1912? Maybe this is not even its date but, rather, that of the incorporation of the Dickson Bridge Works. Perhaps burning off the date was an effort to make people crossing feel safer than they would had they known that the structure was fully a century in age. Would a bridge built for horse-drawn wagons and pedestrians support my SUV? (Of course, rust stains don't send a very reassuring message either.) Or perhaps the bridge has been rebuilt so completely that it is no longer really a 1912 structure at all. Still, the Wight's Island bridge looks like it could be that old. Truss bridges similar to this one were predomi-

Why would anyone choose to burn off the date from the builder-plate on this steel bridge? Wight's Island, Trent River, south of Havelock. (photo courtesy of author)

nant from the 1870s to the 1920s, predated by wooden and iron trusses, and followed increasingly by reinforced concrete. The 1912 used here fits into the proper historical niche.

It is a common Ontario experience to imprint dates on structures that fulfill some sort of public function, or are the expression of a collective achievement. Churches, schools, and municipal buildings are routinely imprinted in this way. Posted dates have the great advantage of providing benchmarks for the age of the neighbourhood and establishing timelines for the use of particular materials and design details. One simply must be cautious as to what any particular date signifies.

Perhaps this episode will encourage readers to start looking at bridges in The Land Between. Begin by keeping an eye out for changes at Wight's Island. Read David Cuming's books on the history of bridges in Ontario. Go to a Northumberland County directory in the Campbellford Public Library and track down details of the Dickson Bridge Works Company. Walk the streets and figure out if the Dickson factory still stands. Think of the vibrancy such an enterprise imparted to the life of a small town that has drifted downward throughout most of living memory. The Wight's Island bridge stands barely fifteen kilometres from where it was manufactured, but imagine the effort to transport it even that short distance to the present site in the horse-and-wagon era. All this field work, and the pleasures of discovering one's locale, is embedded in a rusty, defaced plaque on an old bridge. ■

17. Uranium Yes … Uranium No …

Michèle Proulx

Travelling through a distant corner of Haliburton on Highway 28, past Silent Lake Provincial Park towards Bancroft, watch for a sign for Dyno Road (now County Road 48). Take it! This route passes a small collection of houses that seem to have dropped out of nowhere, a tiny fifteen-lot subdivision in the woods. Welcome to the Dyno Estates, one of the last traces of the uranium boom that visited these parts of The Land Between briefly, about 1960. Those were the days of the onset of the cold war nuclear arms race, and the United States assured its closest trade partner that it would purchase all the uranium Canada could supply.

In the mid-1940s Canada had established the Atomic Energy Control Board

Dyno: will the world's equivocation over nuclear technology allow it to rise again from its ruins, or further fade away to nought but a radioactive scar in The Land Between? (photo courtesy of author)

(AECB), designating uranium as a strategic mineral under federal jurisdiction. Special price contracts allowed for lower grade ore deposits to be considered for development and led to Canada's largest staking blitz up until that time. Among many known uranium deposits found in the Cardiff Township area, Dyno—discovered in November 1953—was one of only four that were developed. In August 1956, AECB awarded Canadian Dyno Mines a special-price contract worth approximately $35 million for 1.2 million kilograms of uranium oxide—more than 2,600 drums—for delivery by March 1963. Mining began in May 1958, and at its peak employed 450 men. They lived in the mine-site bunkhouse, in local summer cottages and in tourist camps. Those with families occupied 50 of the 200 houses built on the Cardiff townsite. Dyno Estates was home for managers and their families.

Then, in an about-face in November 1959, the US Atomic Energy Commission announced that it would terminate purchasing Canadian uranium as of March 1962, effectively eliminating the market for this commodity. Dyno Mine closed in 1960 after less than three years of operation, and the site was abandoned: machinery, housing, waste, everything. At the time there were no requirements to decommission uranium mines. Not until 1977 did AECB assume authority to do remedial work, and then only in response to the persistent pressure of local activists. Dyno Mine site remediation began in 1990, but continued slowly. In 1997 the fine ore bins and mill foundations were still in place, but within a few more years these vestiges had been removed and the entire site covered over with soil. Elevated radiation levels, albeit low, persist.

Canada's uranium industry demonstrates how global politics and federal defence policy can influence the economy, and doubtless the health, of a small, resource-based community of the sort found frequently in The Land Between. The viability of mines is commonly associated with the boom and bust cycle, changes in technology, and the discovery of richer ore bodies, and all of these conspired to sink the Dyno operation and send its people packing. Still, Dyno should be remembered for its lasting contribution to infrastructure. Settlements, highways, churches, and schools throughout the Haliburton and Bancroft parts of The Land Between all are used daily by residents and tourists alike, many of whom have no idea that they are beneficiaries of a mining company.

Dyno should also be remembered as an example of the evolution of mine decommissioning procedures, environmental reclamation technologies, and the influence of thoughtful environmental activists. We have learned, too, that there are finite limits, defined by economy and society, to which such procedures can go. At Dyno low-level radio-activity from waste persists, and people have been hired to provide perpetual monitoring and care. Furthermore, be aware that Dyno may rise again, for the very reasons that it fell: boom and bust, changing technology, the richness of the ore body. This time nuclear power is the market, and uranium prices have multiplied more than ten times over the first decade of the 21st century. Once again, lower grade ore bodies, including several in the Dyno area and others north of Sharbot Lake, are attracting the attention of industrialists and governments. Local activists have, of course, once more been aroused. Remember those fifteen houses dropped in the woods on Dyno Road? Cycles … boom and bust … plus ça change…. ■

18. Riding the Icelanders' Railbed

John S. Marsh

Many railway lines were built in the later 19th century, crossing The Land Between to link southern Ontario and the northern resource frontier. From Lake Simcoe eastward to the Ottawa River Valley all have been abandoned by the trains, but some of the roadbeds have been revived as off-road trails, valuable as recreational, environmental, educational and historic resources.

One such route lies between Lindsay and Haliburton, built as the Victoria Railway between 1874 and 1878. Northward, it passes from farmland on the limestone bedrock to the Canadian Shield, steadily exploited for minerals, forest products, and cottage sites. The Victoria was a lifeline for goods and people in the Haliburton area seeking to be part of the greater Canadian economy and society, a role enhanced by its absorption into the Grand Trunk Railway system in the 1880s, and then into Canadian National Railways in the 1920s. Rail traffic dwindled through the 20th century, thanks to the automobile, and the line closed in 1981.

Today the name of the railroad, and even the concept of being a railroad, has been all but lost under a new brand and 21st-century management structure provided by two separate jurisdictions. From Lindsay to Kinmount, the City of Kawartha Lakes owns and maintains the Victoria Recreation Corridor, fifty-five kilometres of limestone screens and packed earth. At Kinmount the trail meets, seamlessly, the Haliburton Rail Trail, owned by the County of Haliburton, and continues a further thirty-five kilometres on its flat course to the town of Haliburton. Traffic passes for free on foot, bicycle, or horse and, in winter,

Minutes north of Lindsay the Victoria Recreation Corridor—once the Victoria Railway— passes below the abandoned abutment for the bridge that carried another one-time railway across. The short-lived Georgian Bay & Seaboard Railway (1912-1937) was redundant as built, here intersecting another redundant line that has been transformed into a useful recreational element in The Land Between. (photo courtesy of Thomas F. McIlwraith)

on ski or snowmobile. Volunteers take on much of the day-to-day maintenance, picking up litter and trimming bushes. The trail is rough or wet in a few places, but not bad considering that it is no longer maintained to the standards needed for locomotives weighing 120 tonnes or more. And the autumn foliage is spectacular.

To ride the railbed is to embrace The Land Between. Ken Reid Conservation Area, near Lindsay, is 100 hectares with wetlands and woods reached by a floating boardwalk and looped trails; look for nesting ospreys. At Fenelon Falls the swing bridge across the Trent-Severn Waterway stands on its pivot, open and unreachable, a stoic reminder of the railroad origins of the trail. Here the active waterway wins out, and rail trail users deviate across the highway bridge and regain the trail at a sandy beach before proceeding north near the shoreline cottages on Cameron Lake. At Iron Bridge the 1874 structure of that material carried the railway over Burnt River. It was replaced in 1948 with a bridge intended for use in China but not shipped there for political reasons. Users should applaud the Conservation Authority for stepping in before the railway had taken the usual step of salvaging what, for them, was scrap metal when the rails were lifted in the 1980s.

Without bridges the Victoria Rail Trail would not exist.

Pass the 1876 railway station in Kinmount, restored today as a tourist information office and another reminder of the railroad heritage. It is one of the few buildings that survived a devastating fire in 1890. Cross Kendrick's Creek on an intricate wooden trestle. Pause to read the markers in the cemetery at Gelert, a name of Welsh origin. Have a picnic at Ritchie Falls. Contemplate the industrial ruin at Donald, once the site of charcoal, acetate of lime and wood alcohol production. Rail trails invite intimate contact with many aspects of The Land Between.

And so into Haliburton, named for Thomas Chandler Haliburton—judge, land speculator, and mid-19th century author. But do not give him credit for opening up this passage through The Land Between, for he had nothing to do with it. Back a few kilometres, in Kinmount, stands a beautiful memorial with an Icelandic flag. It celebrates the lives of Icelanders who engaged in constructing the railroad in the 1870s. Thereafter, many of them moved on to settle in Manitoba. This old railway route is the Icelanders' legacy, now a green corridor serving new purposes and producing economic benefits they never could have imagined. ∎

The recreation rail trail passes the Austin sawmill on Burnt River at Kinmount. (photo courtesy of John Wadland)

19. Life at Lock 32

Roy T. Bowles & Barbara McFadzen

Samuel de Champlain was the first European clearly identified with The Land Between, and likewise the first to reach the narrows between Sturgeon and Pigeon lakes. For Champlain this was a beautiful woodland spot, and by some accounts he named it accordingly: Beaubocage. That lyrical name, if it had ever caught on, has long since been transformed to today's name: Bobcaygeon. The landscape has evolved too, that beautiful woodland beginning to fall to the axe following survey of the Township of Verulam in 1831. By 1840 several families had settled at Bobcaygeon, some felling trees to make farmland, others felling trees for their own value.

Economic growth in early Bobcaygeon owed much to Mossom Boyd, a descendent of British

Lock 32 in the 1920s was a bucolic place as the Trent-Severn Waterway underwent transition from a commercial to a recreational role in The Land Between. (photograph courtesy of Harry Van Oudenaren)

A busy summer day at Lock 32. (photo courtesy of Roy T. Bowles)

gentry, who arrived in 1833. In 1844 he became manager of a sawmill, soon purchased it and would go on to become "The Lumber King of the Trent Valley." With his sons he expanded the enterprise until Boyd crews were cutting over an extensive area and floating square timber and ships' masts through Bobcaygeon to the St. Lawrence, Quebec, and on to Britain. As the timber trade with Britain declined Boyd established offices in New York State and began shipping sawn lumber there. The Boyd sawmill and stacks of lumber were familiar features of the village until the mill closed in 1904. The Boyds operated steamboats on the Kawartha Lakes and established a sophisticated livestock farm where they experimented with cattalo (a buffalo-cattle cross); through selective breeding they developed the Polled Hereford breed. Boyd family wealth supported many community institutions.

The Trent-Severn Waterway has been important in the development of Bobcaygeon's economic and social life. Charles Poulett Thompson (Lord Sydenham), Governor of the Province of Canada, provided the initiative for its construction; Boyd and other promoters in the region made it a reality. The first lock on the Trent Canal was built at Bobcaygeon in 1833 and a lock capable of passing small steamboats replaced it in 1857. Lake steamers were the primary means of transporting passengers and goods in and out, and helped to establish the tourist industry in The Land Between. Well-to-do visitors from Canada and the United States seeking salubrious air and scenery offered by lakeshore resorts arrived by boat and, beginning in 1904, by rail. Improvements in roads and automobiles after World War II made the pleasures of the area accessible to more people. The steamboats were long gone and by the 1960s the railway was likewise a memory. But the waterway lives on, its shorelines providing attractive locations for resorts, marinas, campgrounds, family summer cottages, and high-amenity year-round homes. Summer vacationers of all ages today crowd Bobcaygeon's streets and businesses, especially around Lock 32, always busy with pleasure boats through the navigation season.

In recent decades, Bobcaygeon has become one of Canada's prime retirement communities and retiring baby boomers are likely to further develop this role. For more than a century the permanent population barely exceeded 1,000 but in the last generation it has nearly tripled. Two-fifths of the population are 65 or older. Many retirees moved from the Toronto area to a community offering enjoyable amenities while retaining reasonable access to the metropolis. Today's Bobcaygeon features new housing projects, several of them labelled "lifestyle communities." Port 32, for instance, is a subdivision of high-quality homes having a private harbour, tennis courts, and recreation centre.

Bobcaygeon celebrates adaptability through time, a persistent theme of The Land Between. The Boyd Heritage Museum, housed in the Company's former office, documents the Boyd family lumbering and other industries as well as their social life. Settlers' Village recalls pioneer life and celebrates it annually with a Settlers' Days event. The many festivals include the spring unlocking of the canal, the fall fair, and the fiddle and step-dance contest. Bobcaygeon's quintessential small-town Ontario streetscape and other retail locations offer a wide range of attractive shopping opportunities including an upscale shoe store with a huge inventory, an award-winning marina, and a dairy popular for its ice cream. Parks, especially along the canal, enhance the experience for residents and visitors.

Bobcaygeon is one of The Land Between's beautiful places. Beaubocage indeed! ■

20. Polly Cow Island

Jane Irwin

Place names imply stories to be told. When a tiny islet at the northerly end of Katchewanooka Lake, near Young's Point, bears the enigmatic name "Polly Cow Island," surely there must be an intriguing story. The Point was named for the Young family who emigrated from Ireland in 1825. Katchewanooka is based on an Ojibwa term meaning "water of many rapids," which indeed it was. But what—or who—was Polly Cow?

The story is that, northeast of Stony Lake there lived, soon after 1800, Handsome Jack Cow, an Ojibwa who "claimed all the streams and lands in this locality as his fishing and hunting grounds." When his daughter, Polly, died at age 16, her grieving father laid her in a birch-bark coffin and led a torch-lit cortège of mourners in canoes to the southernmost of three islands just west of Young's Point. There, on Crown Land, Jack buried Polly Cow beneath a lone balsam fir, digging the grave himself, lining it with stones, and clearing the brush to the shoreline so that her spirit could walk to drink from the rapidly flowing water. During his long period of mourning he camped on the property of

Polly Cow Island is a sacred site in The Land Between, hallowed by both Aboriginal and Western societies. (drawing courtesy of Peterborough Historical Society)

75

his friend, Nathaway Young, close by the island, and visited her grave daily.

Handsome Jack died in 1835, by which time the story of Polly Cow Island had become part of local lore. Newcomers to The Land Between were taking up lots further south along Katchewanooka Lake, among them Catharine Parr Traill, destined to become a distinguished Canadian writer. Throughout her life Catharine took an interest in peoples' life stories, and she regarded their graves as places of memory to be protected. Of roadside burials she wrote: "if the ground was not consecrated, it was hallowed by the tears and prayers of parents and children." She felt deeply the poignancy of "many an unknown grave in Canada long deserted and forgotten." Surely the Polly Cow story was in her mind.

By the 1890s, lakefront lots throughout The Land Between were being marketed as vacation properties. Catharine became concerned that Polly's island might become a cottage lot and her grave, unrecognized, be lost. For any new occupant the name "Polly Cow" would surely be only a puzzle and offer no indication of a sacred place. In 1893 Catharine appealed for help from the well-respected engineer, neighbour, and personal friend, Sandford Fleming. He willingly took up her case with Indian Affairs in Ottawa, the Head of which promptly wrote to Catharine:

"I have the pleasure to inform you that … you will receive a patent for 'Polly Cow's Island.' … It has been a great pleasure to everyone here, from the highest to the lowest official, to do everything in their power to do you honorable service and gratify your every wish—every one of them feeling that the most any of them can do is but the smallest acknowledgment which is due to you for your life-long devotion to Canada."

Hallowed by the tears and prayers of her father and protected by the action of a woman who never knew her in person, Polly's unmarked grave will not be forgotten. Together Handsome Jack Cow and Catharine Parr Traill secured this special place, bridging between Aboriginal and newcomer. Jack's burial place is unknown, whereas Catharine, who died in 1899, lies in consecrated ground at Hillside Cemetery in Lakefield. Catharine's heirs gave the Cow islands to the Peterborough Historical Society, and they—including Polly's grave—are now included in the Trent-Severn Waterway National Historic Site. Catharine's small memorial cairn recalls a Scottish custom of passers-by placing a stone and praying for the soul of the deceased. Imagine those people passing Polly's grave adding their stones to those that Jack had used in lining it so many years before.

Why Jack buried his daughter on Polly Cow Island remains unknown. Was the proximity to Nathaway Young important? Did the rapids of Katchewanooka Lake have a special meaning? For more than 11,000 years the Waterway Lakes have formed an important route for Aboriginal peoples, and they have left many sites along their shores. Polly Cow Island is one more, its full story still untold. ∎

21. An Aquatic Extension of The Land Between

Dana H. Wilson

Consider Georgian Bay, the eastern arm of Lake Huron, as an aquatic extension of The Land Between ecotone. Water, islands, and shoreline straddle the divide between the southern edge of the Canadian Shield and the younger sedimentary rock of the Niagara Escarpment and St. Lawrence Lowlands. It is home to an incredibly wide range of flora and fauna in proportion to the land mass it occupies. Acidic granite runoff from the eastern shores blends with basic limestone influences from the west, allowing for diverse aquatic habitats. Altogether it has a unique ecology.

Glacial features of the Pleistocene Ice Age (roughly 12,000 years ago)

Dolomite limestone cliffs of the Niagara Escarpment on the western shore of Georgian Bay face the granite rocky Shield coastline of the Bay's northeastern shore. The sandy loam beaches of the southern shoreline spread between them. (photos courtesy of author)

dominate the more northerly shoreline of Georgian Bay. Ice action scoured the area, leaving exposed bedrock, gouged-out depressions, and deposits of thick glacial till. The shoreline is rugged, with literally tens of thousands of outcropping islands; on them hardwood forests have grown from the pockets of glacial till. These are the Thirty Thousand Islands, the world's largest freshwater archipelago. Bogs, ponds, and wetlands that have developed from the vacant depressions in the bedrock are also scattered across the northeastern shores.

On the opposite shores of Georgian Bay, younger sedimentary limestone of the Niagara Escarpment rises up to form cliffs along the western coastline that extend north to Tobermory along the Bruce Peninsula. Water levels in Georgian Bay have fluctuated extensively since the last Ice Age causing water action to erode and define the dolomite limestone cliffs along the Escarpment on the western shore. Eroded sedimentary material has been carried south and deposited along the southwestern shores creating beaches of stone and sand.

Nottawasaga Bay is the transitional zone between the rocky granite shores along the east and the limestone cliffs of the Escarpment in the west. Long stretches of sandy beaches formed from the limestone deposits and fine sedimentary material transported from the Nottawasaga River. Wasaga Beach on Nottawasaga Bay is an active sand spit some fourteen kilometres long.

I grew up in this peripheral region of The Land Between, a real transitional area between the boreal forests of the Canadian Shield, and the Niagara Escarpment and hardwood forests in the south. The southern Georgian Bay area is characterized by sand and loamy sand and contains elements of tall grass prairie and pine-oak savannah ecosystems. The area contains an active sand dune system with transverse and parabolic dunes. The blending of the well-defined Shield and Escarpment ecosystems on the east and west regions of Georgian Bay, together with the distinct transition zone along the south, may be grounds for its consideration as an aquatic extension of The Land Between. ∎

22. Carden Plain Alvar:
A Deceptive Landscape

Alan G. Brunger

The alvar is a distinctive ecosystem of The Land Between, most commonly recognized by its level, open, limestone pavement landscape with scattered patches of forest. Of several alvars in The Land Between, the Carden Plain best fits that description. Much of Carden Township (east of Lake Simcoe) comprises limestone plain, partially forested at first survey with some excellent white pine stands; mixed forest now predominates. Settlers in pre-Confederation Ontario, eager to farm the land but inexperienced in reading the landscape, fell prey to unscrupulous Crown agents all too willing to offer these infertile limestone lands for sale. The prospect of being able immediately to obtain unforested land—at least in part—and to plant crops on open meadows, without having to fell trees, must have been most beguiling. Many of these aspiring farmers soon recognized the extraordinary challenge that they faced, however, and left the alvars quickly, although not before they had removed the better timber, mainly pine. Ground strewn with brush was suscep-

Far from being the barrens described in the text, an alvar in springtime is attractive. And so it appears to have been for many early settlers, for whom the thin, droughty land below proved disastrous. (photo courtesy of Couchiching Conservancy)

tible to fires, damaging the characteristically thin and fragile soils. Today's alvars display collapsing rail fences and sagging log buildings, the abandoned artifacts of failed dreams.

Carden Plain, like all alvars, lies atop the northern edge of one of the several Ordovician limestone strata, which gently rise from beneath Lake Ontario and terminate in a long, low, ragged ridge overlooking the southern edge of the Canadian Shield. Vertical cracks have developed along natural joints produced within the rock as it solidified on the tropical coral seafloor hundreds of millennia ago. Slow solution of the lime by weakly acidic rain has gradually produced numerous crevices and holes. Underground streams have enlarged such apertures into caves, awaiting exploration by the intrepid speleologist.

The alvar ecosystem is fragile, scanty flora clinging to thin soil and moist crevices in the limestone. Wood lily, Indian paintbrush, hairy beardtongue, wild bergamot, fragrant sumac, Virginia saxifrage, and balsam ragwort are among the flora able to survive both spring flood and summer drought. A surprising diversity of smaller plants, including moss, lichen, and walking fern grip the almost bare surface and are easily damaged by the wayward footfall. Juniper and white cedar may root deeply within some of these cracks.

Summer bird life in Carden alvar has a northern tone, including the golden-crowned kinglet and water thrush, plus such grassland and shrubland species as bluebirds, bobolinks, whippoorwills, and the endangered loggerhead shrike. Alvars host amphibians and reptiles, particularly garter snakes, and butterflies and dragonflies abound. The relatively breezy openness offers the forest animals relief from biting insects, but exposes the smaller creatures to predators. Conversely, the blasts of winter render the open, unsheltered alvar no place for man or beast.

Years ago alvars were largely rejected as places to live. Population peaked on Carden Plain during the late 19th century lumbering era when local farms supplied produce to nearby lumber camps. In 1881 the Plain supported about 3,300 people on 470 farms; a century later about 1,200 people occupied 100 larger farms covering much less cultivated area. Rough pasture supports beef cattle, but dairying has failed to develop in the Carden Plain.

Despite shortcomings, alvars nevertheless offer spiritual refuge and deserve praise as relatively exclusive places. In 2012 Carden Plain was a candidate for provincial park status. The celebration of its ecological diversity is manifest by events such as the annual Carden Nature Festival. The local Wylie Road is widely recognized as the best early-summer birding road in southern Ontario. Alvars contribute their own particular biodiversity to The Land Between, increasingly resisting encroachment by landholders all too prone to suppose that they are merely the next easy conquest. ■

23. Contacts, Conflicts, Consequences

Brian S. Osborne

For millennia, several groups of Aboriginal people have valued The Land Between as their homeland. At no time was this condition more dynamic than during the 18th century. Following the Huron-Iroquois wars of the 17th century, the Iroquois established settlements and extended their hunting grounds into the lands beyond the north shore of Lake Ontario. In the same period, Nipissing and Algonquin peoples entered the Ottawa River watershed from the north and engaged in what ethnographers speak of as peaceable interaction underpinned by the shared philosophy of *mino bimaadiziwin* (pursuit of the "good life").

Early in the 1700s, however, a series of confrontations commenced between the Mississauga Ojibwa and the Mohawk Iroquois and they are today much a part of the Mississauga mental landscape and place-naming. *Pequahkoondebaminis*, in lower Georgian Bay, was known as the Island of the Skulls because of the "great slaughter" that took place there. *Nogojiwanong*, "the place at the end of the rapids" (Cemetery Point in Peterborough today), witnessed another encounter. Roches Point, on Rice Lake, was the scene of a third battle.

The Mohawk—farming peoples—were thus driven from The Land Between and the Mississauga established themselves in the watersheds of the rivers draining into Lake Ontario. By the late 1700s, Major Robert Rogers of Rogers Rangers (1760) and Colonel John Butler of Butlers Rangers (1779) encountered them in camps along the Bay of Quinte, while Carleton Island became the military base for the Mississauga during the American Revolutionary War. In 1783, the Mississauga ceded lands from the Bay of Quinte to Brockville and as far inland as a "man could travel in a day." Five years later they ceded lands from the Bay of Quinte to York (Toronto) and inland as far as the "sound of a gunshot." However vaguely defined, this huge tract of land accommodated the United Empire Loyalists displaced from the United States, although territory to the rear continued to be used by the Mississauga as their traditional homeland. Throughout the first half of the 19th century, settlement and resource extraction drew Europeans ever deeper into the interior, provoking renewed pressures on Mississauga lands. Again the British stepped in and, in 1822, concluded a treaty over some 2.7 million acres (1.1 million hectares) more, extending

The war memorial on the Alderville F. N. reserve at Alnwick remembers Mississaugas who served in the Great War.

between the Ottawa River and Georgian Bay: the core of The Land Between.

The Mississauga made two strategic responses to these disruptions. One was religious. After hearing the preaching of Peter Jones (*Kahkewaquonaby*), a young man of mixed Mississauga and Welsh ancestry, a number of Mississauga in the Kingston and Bay of Quinte areas converted to Methodism in 1826. They established a new agricultural village on Grape Island in the Bay of Quinte the following year, with a church, school, and houses, and they devoted themselves to producing crops and livestock. It became increasingly clear, however, that Grape Island was too small, and hence the Mississauga appealed to the Crown for more land. Their preference was for "somewhere back between the River Trent & Rice Lake where the white people have not settled on." Choosing not to join existing Mississauga villages at Rice Lake, in 1835 the Grape Island community succeeded in having the Crown lay out sixteen fifty-acre (twenty-hectare) homesteads on the south side of Rice Lake in Alnwick Township. Apparently their interest in farming was sustained.

The second Mississauga strategy was to resume their traditional lifestyle. Not all members had been enamoured with Methodism or attracted by life on Grape Island, and some continued to seek the freedom of the bush. In 1831, the Crown granted them 2,680 acres (nearly 1,100 hectares) in nineteen lots on Wolfe Lake in Bedford Township, about halfway between Kingston and Perth, at the eastern end of The Land Between. There they briefly pursued a way of living that included receiving the traditional annual government gifts of guns and traps rather than plows and seed. But, in 1836, this experiment was terminated, the Mississauga ceded their Bedford lands to the Crown, and while some of them retreated deeper into the as-yet unsurveyed lands to the north, the majority rejoined their kin on the Alderville reserve in Alnwick.

Here the Mississauga of Kingston and Bay of Quinte reside today, in a landscape of drumlinized till-land lying at the southern edge of The Land Between. The dramatic odyssey of the Alderville residents is a signal demonstration of their long history of interaction between The Land Between and the lands to the south. Perhaps the most evocative symbols of this relationship are the Methodist Church at Alderville and the memorial there to the Mississaugas' service in the First World War. ■

24. Enlightened Minds and Muskies at Nogies Creek

Tom Whillans

During the late 19th century overseers for the Federal Department of Marine and Fisheries reported huge commercial landings of fish in the reservoirs known as the Kawartha Lakes and the contiguous waters of the Otonabee River system. Lake Scugog supported a prodigious fishery for maskinonge (muskellunge). Stony Lake was renowned for its salmon trout (lake trout). The Land Between was teeming with fish. Through the early years of the 20th century, just when the focus of the Kawartha waters shifted from commercial transportation to recreational boating, The Land Between rapidly became a popular destination for anglers.

By the 1930s, however, stocks were shrinking and alarm bells began to sound. The Ontario Federation of Anglers had become sufficiently concerned about the decline of the muskellunge in the Kawartha Lakes that, in 1937, it engaged respected ichthyologists from the University of Toronto and Queen's University in Kingston to investigate. Professor J. R.

Ed Crossman and Tom Whillans insert an ultrasound transmitter in an anaesthetized muskellunge at the Nogies Creek field research laboratory, 1974. (photo courtesy of Fergus McNeill)

Dymond of this group was also a founding member of the Federation of Ontario Naturalists in 1932, evidence of an awakening in public concern for natural history and habitats. The Ontario government signalled its support by establishing the Ontario Fisheries Research Laboratory (OFRL) at this time, recognizing the economic potential of a healthy recreational fishery.

Following World War II, F. E. J. Fry of OFRL approached the influential Toronto Anglers and Hunters Association and, buoyed with funds from the Canadian National Sportsmen's Show, in 1951 founded a research station at the provincial fish sanctuary at Nogies Creek, upstream from its outfall into Pigeon Lake. I cannot help thinking that the hand of Leslie Frost was very close, he being from Lindsay and always a champion and sympathetic voice for the Kawartha region.

Nogies Creek research station was dedicated to the conservation of muskellunge. Fry was the principal scientist there for nearly twenty years, and muskellunge biology was the initial research focus. Projects that followed included the stocking of muskellunge fingerlings and experiments in the transfer of adult fish. Subsequent projects supervised by Fry's successor, Ed Crossman, included muskellunge ecology and angling stress. Largemouth bass biology, painted turtles, wetland ecology, and bullfrogs all drew attention, and students and faculty from Trent University became increasingly involved. During its 37 years of operation, Nogies Creek research involved over 30 scientists and students, resulted in approximately 10 graduate degrees, some 40 scientific publications, 42 newspaper articles, and more than a dozen radio and television pieces. At the height of scientific activity between 1974 and 1980, the station entertained approximately 2,300 visitors. It was a wonderful point for science and the public to converge, challenging the ivory tower image of academe.

And the muskellunge? At the moment the species remains abundant in the Kawartha Lakes, but it has led a charmed existence. Its close relative, the northern pike, is not native to the Kawarthas, but has been invading from the north through the canal system. By the summer of 2010 it was reproducing as far downstream as Balsam Lake. Where the two species coexist, muskellunge tend to fare poorly. Thus, the great lunge's future is cloudy. If it is to survive, the knowledge available to managers from the research at Nogies Creek will surely prove invaluable.

Nogies Creek research station closed in 1988, to re-emerge a decade later in a new style suited to the 21st century. In 1998 Marjorie Oliver donated to Trent University her family homestead on 270 acres (109 hectares) along the north shore of Pigeon Lake, near the outfall of Nogies Creek and within a few minutes driving from the site of the research station. Led by professors in the Environmental and Resource Studies Program and Biology Department at Trent, the property was developed into the James McLean Oliver Ecological Centre, named after Marjorie's father. Research projects have resulted in fifty-nine publications and theses; these address exotic, native and invasive fish, fish habitat restoration, airborne pollutants, environmental monitoring methods, flying squirrels, saw-whet owls migration, nutrient impacts on aquatic conditions, and biogas. Vegetational succession and climate change are harbingers of a new era of research that bridges aquatic, terrestrial, and atmospheric issues.

In 2003, shortly before he died, Ed Crossman transferred to the Oliver Ecological Centre the records of the Nogies Creek Research Station, the baton of an ichthylogical research legacy for the benefit of anglers and others in The Land Between. ∎

25. Love Letters from the Western Islands

Claire Elizabeth Campbell

A.Y. Jackson had long loved the Georgian Bay. By 1931, at forty-nine years old, he had been visiting it for over twenty years, drawn by the stark silhouettes of bent white pine and the glowing rose granite of the Canadian Shield. With the rest of the Group of Seven, he had made the Bay into one of Canada's most famous landscapes, through paintings like *Terre Sauvage* (1913) and *Night, Pine Island* (1921). But he wanted someone else to see it.

A.Y. Jackson, "Boat and Tent at Night, Western Islands" *(1933). (courtesy National Gallery of Canada)*

"Pine Island is the place I want to take you some day. Do you like it?"

St. Joachim, 22 March, 1932

In a box in the National Archives sits a pile of letters from Jackson to Anne Savage, a renowned artist and teacher in Montreal. In 1931, Jackson began pestering Savage to join him in the Bay, sometimes writing by the light of campfires on the islands. He promised her inspirational landscapes for painting, told her of picnicking and painting trips, and regaled her with stories of his misadventures in a fairly isolated archipelago. "I had a tube of permanent blue," he told her in 1933, "[but] it was ivory black labelled wrongly and a twenty-five mile row to town, so I had to avoid blue subjects."

But it was the Westerns he promised her, and it was on the Westerns that he knew he was in love. He had been there a few times before, sometimes with friends who had a cottage in Go-Home Bay.

"The Westerns are a little group of rocks and islands far out on the Georgian Bay, wild, wind swept. … One of the islands is covered with pine, but most of them are bare rocks. … No one ever seems to go there. It should be a great place to sketch … and I will do everything I can to make you happy. So there you are dear."

Toronto, 28 June, 1933

Anne agreed to join him in July of 1933. She took the train from Toronto, and they headed far out into the open Bay to the remote island group, and sketched. After she left, he praised her work of the "little pool" (what would become *Dark Pool, Georgian Bay*) and the twisted pines. He would paddle out to the open and gaze at the Western Islands, lost in thought.

Sixty-five years later, I sat in the archives holding faded, penciled letters from one of Canada's most famous artists, describing a place with all the passion I had come to expect of people who knew and loved the "wild, woolly" Georgian Bay, the western fringe of our Land Between. But suddenly I was reading not the notes of an inspired artist, but the private pleas of a man. It seemed almost rude to pry. His letters became as bare as the island rock. "There are an awful lot of lakes up here, and I would like to paddle you through all of them," he wrote, a little desperately, a few weeks after she left. "And make pancakes for you and coffee, and shelter you against wind and rain and sun, you dear serene soul."

Finally there was nowhere left to go.

"You are the dearest and sweetest soul I know, and if you will be my wife I will try so much to make you happy... when I wanted so much to tell you I loved you out on the Western Islands the words would not come…. Tell me what to do and I'll try to make good and be worthy of your affection. As ever, Alex."

Toronto, 7 September, 1933

Neither Jackson nor Savage ever married, though they wrote to each other all their lives. ∎

26. Ghosts of Grain and Timber

Ron Brown

A walk through the young forests of the Ojibwa First Nation lands on Parry Island seems pretty much like any other walk in the woods … that is, until the old rutted road comes to a clearing and there, rising above the brush, loom the Roman-like ruins of a roofless railway roundhouse. Further on, the trail leads along what were once cindered roads past more than a hundred overgrown foundations. Over the granite ridge, the waters of Georgian Bay lap against the docks which once held massive grain elevators. For more than a quarter of a century, Depot Harbour rivalled Collingwood, Midland, and Port McNicoll. Today, all is ghostly silence.

It all began with one of Canada's most ambitious railway builders, John Rudolphus Booth. Determined to build an empire on shipping lumber and grain, Booth rose from his Quebec farm roots to create a prosperous sawmilling business in Ottawa. After acquiring lush timber limits in the 1880s in what would become Algonquin Park a decade later, he

On Parry Island, the landscape of the Precambrian Shield gradually consumes the roundhouse of the Canada Atlantic Railway, an artifact from a brief industrial interlude in The Land Between. (photo courtesy of author)

proceeded to build the Canada Atlantic Railway, to ship out the wood, mill it in the nation's capital, and send it on to New England markets.

Unlike the Trent-Severn Waterway, which received and forwarded timber flushed down the many streams in The Land Between, Booth's railway cut across the headwaters and carried the timber out the back door, as it were, bypassing The Land Between on the north. This initiative surely deprived The Land Between of resource income for a number of decades, but it may also have preserved the area for its much more enduring recreational role.

His ambition yet unfulfilled, Booth extended his railway westward, beyond the most prolific forests, through The Land Between to Georgian Bay. His goal was Parry Island, one of the Bay's estimated 30,000 islands and site of one of the very best harbours to be found anywhere on the Great Lakes. Wide, protected, and deep right to the shore, Depot Harbour could easily accommodate not only timber vessels, but also the largest grain boats, while the level backshore was an ideal townsite. Booth, the timber baron, was entering the prairie grain trade.

Begun in 1895, Depot Harbour grew along a network of streets, with hotels, boarding houses, three churches, a school and 110 family homes. Two massive grain elevators loomed over the water while rail yards, a watering tower, and station saw trains departing as frequently as every twenty minutes at peak periods. A swing bridge across a narrow channel made Parry Island truly part of the mainland. Booth and the Ojibwa Nation had nego- tiated all this development, but when prosperity determined that he needed additional land, Booth high-handedly invoked a clause in the Railway Act and expropriated it. Legal action by the Ojibwa proved fruitless and the animosity still resonates.

For nearly forty years Depot Harbour, The Land Between's own port, continued to be among the busiest on the Great Lakes. But its time was running out. The last trainload of timber headed eastward from Rock Lake along Booth's railway in 1925, leaving grain in transit as the sole traffic. This part of The Land Between generated virtually no local railway traffic, and was poised to become a prime attraction for the automobile-oriented cottage world. In 1933, at the height of the Depression, ice destroyed a trestle in Algonquin Park, severing the rail route. Suddenly, and irrevocably, Depot Harbour had lost its reason for existing. Fire destroyed the empty grain elevators in 1945, and by 1953, the long-vacant houses had been sold and removed.

Across The Land Between the rails of Booth's railway were lifted late in the 1950s, the abandoned roadbed leaving only a faint trace through places like Edgington and Seguin Falls. Forest has gradu- ally reclaimed the Depot Harbour townsite, and ownership of the land has returned to the Ojibwa. The wharves remain, and the wooden pilings of the coal dock protrude above the waters. On a rocky knoll overlooking the bay, broken steps lead up to the ruins of the Catholic church. Crumbling sidewalks pass collapsing foundations. And there, rising above the brush, loom the Roman-like ruins of a roofless railway roundhouse. ■

Depot Harbour, viewed from the grain elevator. The Canada Atlantic Railway roundhouse is visible in the right centre. (courtesy Archives of Ontario, Daniel T. Thomas Collection, C253, tray 5, image 16)

27. Navigating The Land Between

Dennis Carter-Edwards

The Trent-Severn Waterway, connecting Lake Ontario with Georgian Bay, is a major arterial route through The Land Between. Built gradually over a period of eighty-seven years, between 1833 and 1920, it might properly be called The Land Between Waterway, for more than two-thirds of its length lies within the ecological region featured in this book. Furthermore, for most of the century following the initial survey by Scottish engineer Nicol Hugh Baird, leading to construction of the first lock at Bobcaygeon in the 1830s, the project was clearly centred locally within The Land Between. Much of the work consisted of flooding out rapids with wooden dams, which created power sites for mills, and building locks—first masonry and later concrete—that permitted navigation. Agricultural settlement was the dream. During the 1840s locks were added as far west as Lindsay and a series of timber slides were constructed to support the region's expanding forest industry. This combination of power and mobility within a single waterway system has rarely been matched in Ontario.

After Confederation, the Province of Ontario extended the canal into Balsam Lake. This project was, again, simply a local initiative intended to support regional economic development. By the 1880s the Federal government had become deeply involved, building more locks, but these too were intended to serve strictly regional interests. Rather than promote a through system of navigation between Lake Ontario and Georgian Bay,

The Land Between cuts a broad swath through the area drained by the Trent-Severn Waterway. This map shows the extent to which this ecotone of diversity is influenced by circumstances well beyond its perceived limits.

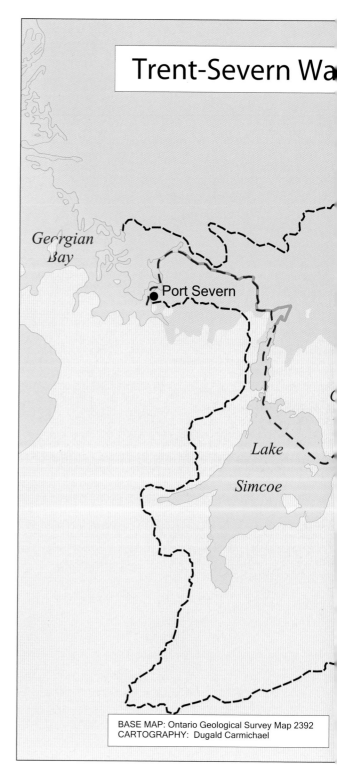

Trent-Severn Wa...

Georgian Bay

● Port Severn

Lake Simcoe

BASE MAP: Ontario Geological Survey Map 2392
CARTOGRAPHY: Dugald Carmichael

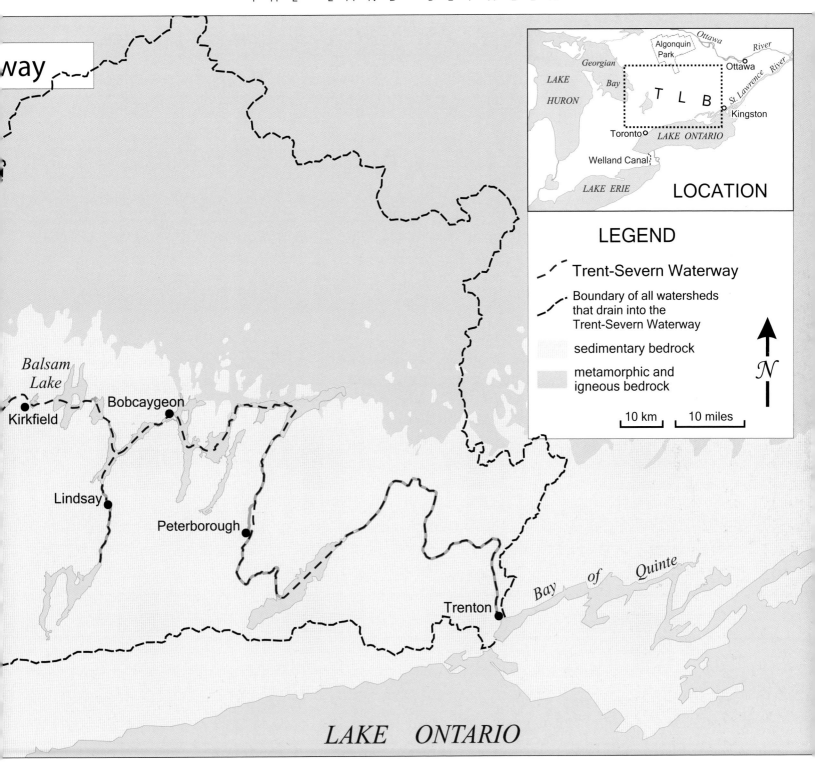

the early Trent Canal was still very much a creature of The Land Between. The "Severn" part was still in the future.

The turning point came just before the 1891 national election when the Conservative Government of Sir John A. Macdonald committed itself to extending the water route onward to Lake Simcoe. The waterway was to be a link in a larger scheme, a barge passage carrying prairie wheat across central Ontario and avoiding the circuitous route through Lake Erie and the Welland Canal. Gaps in the Trent Canal north of Peterborough and east of Lake Simcoe would be closed (although railways had already done so twenty years previously). Included in this construction program were two landmark engineering works, hydraulic lift locks at Peterborough and Kirkfield, and the first Canadian use of concrete in lock construction. The last link, between Lake Simcoe and Georgian Bay, was authorized in 1912. By this time, however, the notion of a barge canal for wheat had given way to visions of tourism. When the through route was finally opened in 1920 it was a pleasure boat, the *Irene*, which was the first to sail through from Trenton to Port Severn. No sooner had nationwide commerce been made possible than it was overtaken by recreational boating through this picturesque section of Ontario.

The Trent-Severn Waterway has had a major impact on the cultural and natural landscape of The Land Between. Consider Canal Lake, on the section between Lake Simcoe and Balsam Lake. It was a shallow, narrow stretch of water until the coming of the canal, at which time it was flooded to provide for both navigation and water supply. Throughout the Trent-Severn system, dams and reservoir lakes have re-engineered the landscape, creating a complex water management regime and establishing new ecosystems.

Today Parks Canada operates the Waterway, which was designated an historic site in 1929. Lock stations are hubs of recreational and tourism activity, energizing the economy and lifestyle of numerous communities. In addition to providing safe and efficient navigation, Parks Canada plays an important environmental management role, offering memorable experiences and heritage presentations to boaters and land-based visitors. ■

28. Cold-Blooded Treasures of The Land Between

Doug Armstrong

As a child I spent much of our family holidays on Kushog Lake searching for reptiles and amphibians. Part of the fascination with reptiles was that they were hard to find. Although ring-necked snakes and garter snakes turned up regularly in the old fields of Walker's Farm, the others were less forthcoming. I recall my only glimpse of a water snake in 1968, and many years elapsed before my first sighting of the cryptic (but probably common) green snake in 1980. Although painted turtles are common, by the time we got to the cottage they were extremely hard to see amongst the thick pondweed in the marsh. I was especially delighted to find my first snapping turtle in the adjoining Sherbourne Lake, and even more so when they later started turning up in Kushog.

The term "reptile" is unfortunate, as it is a Greek translation of "creepy crawly" that was originally used to refer to just about any type of animal deemed objectionable. Today it is used to describe four different groups of "cold-blooded" land-living animals with backbones. More correctly, they are exothermic, meaning that they get their heat from the outside environment rather than from their metabolism. Consequently, reptiles are often seen basking in the sun, frequently

The snapping turtle has been given a bad reputation when all it is doing is defending itself on land. It does not snap under water.

Seven turtle species share The Land Between with the thirteen squamates. Four other species are largely confined to the Carolinian zone of the southern tip of Ontario, a region that has all 24 of Ontario's reptiles but at very low numbers due to habitat loss. The number of reptile species drops off quickly north from The Land Between, to nine north of Lake Huron and only one—the eastern garter snake—in the boreal region. The Land Between can be considered to have an in-between reptile fauna, just as it is in-between in its geology and general ecology.

on warm surfaces such as the limestone and granite outcrops that are so common in The Land Between.

The Land Between is home to two of the four groups of reptiles: the squamates (lizards and snakes) and the chelonians (turtles). Snakes are actually a type of lizard rather than something separate, and are not even the only group of legless lizards. However, they get their own common name because there are so many of them. The Land Between has twelve snake species and only a single non-snake lizard. The latter is the five-lined skink, whose Ontario range is almost entirely confined to The Land Between, due to decline in the Carolinian zone. The most striking thing about these little jewels is the bright blue tail which is only found on juveniles. The tail presents an inviting target for predators, but breaks off when grabbed, sparing the lizard. I once scared a juvenile that ran into a hole but left its tail hanging out, making it seem as if I was being dared to pull it off.

COSSARO (Committee On the Status of Species At Risk in Ontario) has placed most reptiles in The Land Between on watch. Two are considered endangered (spotted turtle, wood turtle), six threatened (stinkpot turtle, Blanding's turtle, eastern hognose snake, eastern fox snake, gray rat snake, Massasauga rattlesnake), and five "of special concern" (snapping turtle, northern map turtle, five-lined skink, northern ribbon snake,

eastern milk snake). Loss and degradation of habitat is the most obvious threat, but reptile populations are surprisingly sensitive to the deaths of adult animals. Decline can result from animals being taken away as pets or being killed by vehicles or boat propellers. Snapping turtles and rattlesnakes are subject to deliberate persecution. Ironically it is the long lifespans of many reptiles that make them so vulnerable.

Turtles, in particular, are famous for their long lives, and I imagine them spending happy decades of quiet philosophical musing on their favourite basking logs. Turtles have "negligible senescence," meaning there is no indication that they ever grow old. They keep going until bad luck strikes—accident, disease, or predator—and this may be a very long time for a large animal protected by a bony shell. Research suggests that many snapping turtles live for more than a century and that it may not be uncommon for them

to reach 200 years of age. Population stability depends on this longevity due to the poor survival of eggs and young, particularly in northern locations like The Land Between. Even low levels of adult mortality can drive populations slowly toward extinction without anyone noticing.

Female turtles in The Land Between are especially vulnerable when migrating between roadside ponds and upland nesting sites in the spring. If you see a turtle crossing the road, please offer help. You need to avoid the front end of snapping turtles for obvious reasons, but can carry them safely by gripping the rear end of the carapace (upper shell) on either side of the tail. The hissing and snapping may suggest a lack of gratitude, but these normally good-natured animals are just trying to defend themselves. And they may thank you later during another hundred years of quiet contemplation on their favourite basking log. ∎

This five-lined skink has its full tail easily shed if chased by a predator.

29. Al Purdy's Back Country

Gordon Johnston

Al Purdy's "The Country North of Belleville" won an award in 1963 for best poem of the year, and since then it has been generally regarded as one of his masterpieces. So closely is it identified with him that we think of the landscape as his when, in fact, he lived south of Belleville, in Prince Edward County. The poem's terrain is the country first opened up by the Colonization Roads built in the middle of the 19th century at a time when it was commonly believed that pine forest land was good for farming and that snow fertilized the soil. The townships were named at the time mostly for towns in Ireland and for British scientists.

And the place now seems central to our imaginations because this is where the colonizers' dream of transplanting the British Isles reached its limit, where character and the imagination are tested. The thin soil scraped from the Shield would not quite support agriculture; our human geometries have dissolved back into the wilderness. The poem is balanced perfectly on this tipping point in geography, and in history; this is also that point in time when the younger generation turned away from farming and headed to the cities.

Purdy was both a traveller and a homebody; his poem is about choosing to stay or to go. The choice defines us all. Are we field scientists like the astronomer Sir John Frederick William Herschel, or laboratory scientists like William Hyde Wollaston or Michael Faraday? Are we hikers, or couch potatoes?

Purdy probably chose these names and the others for their rhythms, their poetic sounds. Here at last, in 1963, were names not from across the Atlantic but from a place adjacent to where we lived, a place at the same time familiar and exotic. The poem's shape is inextricable from what it says. With its stops and starts, its sudden turns, it enacts the difficulties both of plowing in such fields and of thinking about those fields. It even provides a moving image for that deep congruence of inner and outer realities, of the parallel convolutions in the farmer's brain. And it pivots as Purdy poems often do, in the middle: "and yet" it says, at the turning point. His perfect blend of comedy, sentiment, and ironic

North of Belleville spreads a landscape of tenuous promise. Clear the stones, cut the trees, build a well-nogged house, plant a field— and then, all too frequently, lament the miserliness of it all and walk away. Rawdon Township. (photos courtesy of Thomas F. McIlwraith)

understated regret takes us directly to the heart of The Land Between. And there is a wonderful poetic rightness in the fact (as he tells us in a later poem, called "An Arrogance") that he clad the house he built in Roblin Lake with barn board he found in the country north of Belleville. We may not live there, but we house ourselves in what we find there.

THE COUNTRY NORTH OF BELLEVILLE

Bush land and scrub land—
    Cashel Township and Wollaston
Elzevir McClure and Dungannon
green lands of Weslemkoon Lake
where a man might have some
    opinion of what beauty
is and none deny him
    for miles—

Yet this is the country of defeat
where Sisyphus rolls a big stone
year after year up the ancient hills
picnicking glaciers have left strewn
with centuries' rubble
    backbreaking days
    in the sun and rain
when realization seeps slow in the mind
without grandeur or self deception in
    noble struggle
of being a fool—

A country of quiescence and still distance
a lean land
    not like the fat south
with inches of black soil on
    Earth's round belly—
And where the farms are
    it's as if a man stuck

both thumbs in the stony earth and pulled
    it apart
    to make room
enough between the trees
for a wife
    and maybe some cows and
    room for some
of the more easily kept illusions—
And when the farms have gone back
to forest
    are only soft outlines
    shadowy differences—

Old fences drift vaguely among the trees
    a pile of moss-covered stones
gathered for some ghost purpose
has lost meaning under the meaningless sky
    —they are like cities under water
and the undulating green waves of time
    are laid on them—

This is the country of our defeat
    and yet
during the fall plowing a man
might stop and stand in a brown valley
    of the furrows
    and shade his eyes to watch for the same
    red patch mixed with gold

that appears on the same
    spot in the hills
    year after year
    and grow old
plowing and plowing a ten-acre field until
the convolutions run parallel with his own brain—

And this is a country where the young
    leave quickly
unwilling to know what their fathers know
or think the words their mothers do not say—

Herschel Monteagle and Faraday
lakeland rockland and hill country
a little adjacent to where the world is
a little north of where the cities are and
sometime
we may go back there
    to the country of our defeat
Wollaston Elzevir and Dungannon
and Weslemkoon lake land
where the high townships of Cashel
    McClure and Marmora once were—
But it's been a long time since
and we must enquire the way
    of strangers— ■

30. Fire!

Brian S. Osborne

Fire has long been a major presence in The Land Between. Whether started by lightning or Native peoples, pre-historic forests have adjusted to periodic burnover. The advent of European settlers, however, has forever changed the relationship between humans and woodland. Motivated by economics to exploit resources and attempt farming, settlers were also driven by a deep-seated and long-standing antipathy to the forest. For millennia, Europeans had considered it as a wilderness, an obstacle to the development of a cultivated place.

Fire as destruction. The black-and-white image by an anonymous photographer captures the destructive power of fire. (courtesy of Rory MacKay)

Consider the pyromaniacal reactions of Posthuma Simcoe, wife of the first Lieutenant Governor of Upper Canada. Writing in her diary in 1792, she ponders whether her reader can imagine "the pleasure of walking in a burning wood." She concludes that "I think I shall have some woods set on fire for my Evening walks." Her rationale was clear. Pragmatically, the smoke "keeps the Musquitoes at a distance," and aesthetically, "where the fire has caught the hollow trunk of a lofty Tree the flame issuing from the top has a fine effect." Little had changed more than forty years later, when another English traveller, Anna Jameson, observed that a "Canadian settler hates a tree, regards it as his natural enemy, as something to be destroyed, eradicated, annihilated by all and any means."

With the passage of the Public Lands and Colonization Roads Act (1853) and the Free Grant and Homestead Act (1868), these attitudes spread into The Land Between. Lumbering and agricultural settlement expanded, and so did the frequency of fires. Cut-over timberland covered with brush was particularly susceptible. Pioneer slash-and-burn practices were an added threat. It was even charged that mineral prospectors deliberately set fires to facilitate their search for profitable deposits. When railways penetrated The Land Between after Confederation, sparks from the wood-burning steam engines became an additional cause of forest fires.

The impacts defy comprehension. In the summer of 1881, Kingston's *British Whig* reported that citizens could smell forest fires burning to the north. Within weeks, the fires had become "too numerous to count and they are to be found in all directions, causing a volume of smoke which has drifted to and hangs heavily over the city … so black as to obscure the sun," even disrupting St. Lawrence River navigation. By the end of September, the fires had been burning for some six weeks throughout Kingston's back country and the townships of Clarendon and Miller had been "swept over by the fiery scourge carrying destitution and loss," while Canonto was described as "a smouldering fire bed." The *Montreal Witness* added that "it is very hard for the Canadian to realize the state of things which is approaching, so long has it been to contend with the forest that we look upon it rather as an enemy than a friend." Shades of Anna Jameson!

By the late 19th century, sentiments were changing. A growing awareness of the waste ensuing from unregulated cutting led to a call in 1882 for "experts and scientific men, to take stock of our forest wealth." In 1899, an Ontario Royal Commission recommended the establishment of forest reserves, leading to legislation whereby lands "deemed suitable for the purposes of future timber supplies [should be] kept in a state of nature as nearly as possible." The first reserve protected some 80,000 acres (33,000 hectares) of The Land Between forest in the rear of Frontenac and Lennox & Addington.

Further, "Algonquin National Park of Ontario" was established in 1893 and promoted "as a public park and forest reservation, fish and game preserve, health resort and pleasure ground for the benefit, advantage and enjoyment of the people of the Province." Ontario's "wilderness" was increasingly being marketed as a place of sanctuary and recreation as contemporary commentators castigated the isolated, monotonous, artificial, and unhealthy life of cities. In "An Invitation to the Woods," poet Archibald Lampman asks Canadians if they are "broke with the din of the streets [and] bowed and bended double with a weight of care and trouble?" For him, the answer was to "take your body and soul to the woods, to the tonic and control of its moods, where the forest gleams and quivers." But it neither gleamed nor quivered if burned out.

Resort hotels, cottages, and summer camps invaded the woods and lakes from Georgian Bay to the Ottawa River, stretching along the Frontenac Arch to the Thousand Islands. Rational resource management policies recognized that nature contributed to the physical and psychic health of society. Initially a simplistic eugenics-driven thesis, this idealistic concern for nature was reinforced by ethical and aesthetic reasoning. Indeed, the dramatic fires that had ravaged The Land Between in the late 19th century may have served as beacons, drawing attention to the need for a more practical and sensitive policy of forest management and engagement with nature. ■

In "Fire Swept Algoma" (1920), Franz (Frank) Johnston depicts the devastation of the ever-present threat of fire. (courtesy National Gallery of Canada)

31. Sustainable Forestry Is Alive in The Land Between

Nathan Basiliko

Across Canada forestry is in sharp decline. While global competition and various legacies of mismanagement have led to the closure of many saw-log and pulp mills in Ontario and Quebec, one forestry company opened a mill in The Land Between in 2009 and is in the initial stages of producing bioenergy with wood "waste." This company logs with horses when working in ecologically sensitive areas ... and is turning a profit! The modern-day Haliburton Forest and Wildlife Preserve is a testament to the benefits of doing things right over the long term. Haliburton Forest, located

Modern skidders and draft horses are among the tools used on the Haliburton Forest and Wildlife Reserve Limited to help meet its sustainable forestry mandate. (photo courtesy of Dr Peter Schleifenbaum)

The Hawk Lake Log Chute north of Carnarvon – a restoration for display purposes – represents an alternative means of moving logs.

south of Algonquin Park, covers more than 60,000 acres (24,000 hectares). It is Ontario's largest privately-owned piece of land and the largest private woodlot in the province. Haliburton Forest was also the very first Canadian forestry company to earn accreditation by the Forest Stewardship Council for carrying out sustainable forestry, a designation recognized by Greenpeace.

Like most forest land in southern Ontario, the land that was to become Haliburton Forest in 1987 had been severely high-graded, a process in which large valuable trees, often of a single species, are selectively removed. Although profitable in the short term, high-grading leaves behind ecologically unhealthy forests and reduces future value, both economic and social. Active conservation guided by cutting-edge scientific practices over the past four decades has, however, restored the functioning and value of the forest ecosystems at Haliburton. Forests are now harvested selectively; that is, only a limited percentage of trees are logged, and foresters arrange to avoid the old procedure of removing only the healthy, large trees of one species. This strategy has resulted in a diverse, healthy, and beautiful forest that successfully supports outdoor activities such as camping, hiking, cycling, hunting, snowmobiling, and fishing side-by-side with forestry operations. Haliburton Forest is also the site of a well-respected wolf preserve and research centre. Numerous long-term ecological research projects are underway in conjunction with the University of Toronto.

The future of forestry in The Land Between is greener than ever. In the context of dwindling Canadian pulp markets and burgeoning energy markets, Haliburton Forest is currently developing its own on-site energy generator adjacent to its new lumber mill. Woodchips and sawdust that in the past, have been shipped away by fuel-guzzling trucks and eventually made into paper, will now be "gasified" under high temperature and low oxygen conditions. The result is a biofuel of hydrogen and methane gas, cleanly produced, that can be used to fuel nearby kilns, buildings, and generators. The by-product, charcoal, is spread back into the forest soils to improve forest nutrition and keep the biofuel production cycle sustainable. With poignant controversy surrounding the production of biofuels from cropland needed to grow food, Canada's forests may hold one of the solutions to dealing with our heavy reliance on climate-warming fossil fuels. The local scale of forest biomass and bioenergy production on the Haliburton site also greatly reduces fuel consumption and enhances the net benefit of biofuel production.

Innovation and diversification set in a classic natural Ontario setting undoubtedly has placed Haliburton Forest apart as a model for the future of Canadian forestry. It is a fine element in the biological and social diversity of The Land Between. ■

32. A Stonemason of English Predilections

Laurel Sefton MacDowell

Near Carnarvon in old Stanhope Township (now Algonquin Highlands Township), St. Peter's, a small Anglican church, stands amidst the wooded landscape punctured with fragments of the Canadian Shield. Built of granite in 1906, St. Peter's survived tornadoes in 2006, its century year, and still holds services for the local community every Sunday year round. A source of pride in the small community, it is the best-known building of Haliburton stonemason John Henry Billing.

Two alleged characteristics of local people in Haliburton County are their strong streaks of individualism and their cheerful non-conformity. John Billing, a pioneer settler, possessed both traits in abundance. Though very much an Englishman, naming his home and church after those in his birthplace, he became thoroughly Canadian once he was working in his new environment. Local building materials helped connect him to his new community. In Ontario's logging country he built in stone, which was unusual, and

In the timber limits of The Land Between, stonemason John Henry Billing chose not to build in wood, as his neighbours did, but, rather, in stone. St. Peter's Anglican Church near Carnarvon shows off the fine talent he learned in his youth in England. (photo courtesy of the author)

his distinctive granite buildings are his legacy. They include his gabled, Victorian home—Blagdon Hill—overlooking the surrounding lakes; it is currently owned by the heirs of renowned architect B. Napier Simpson, Jr., who purchased it in 1954 and subsequently restored it.

Born in 1838 in Blagdon Hill, Somerset, John Billing became a stonemason and built a wall in his village, restored Pitminster church, and worked on the Clifton suspension bridge in Bristol. As a young adult he caught malarial fever and, needing a change of climate, in 1870 sailed to Canada with his wife, Charity Wood Billing. Residing briefly in Sutton, Quebec, and in Chicago, they eventually settled in Toronto where John worked on various projects, including the tower and spire of St. James' Cathedral, a stone bridge over the Humber River, and a monument and wall at Howard Park. When his fever returned, Billing moved northwards, finding employment on the Victoria Railway, then building its line towards Haliburton and wintering in a camp in the remote Township of Stanhope.

Billing received a free land grant of 100 acres (about 40 hectares) "wholly unoccupied and unimproved" in Stanhope in 1876. He swore that he was not interested in the minerals or timber; instead he built what local people referred to as the old Billing road, along which companies for years hauled logs. From the road he climbed up the hill to his "estate" and developed "Hillcrest farm." Later he obtained a second grant of 200 acres (about 80 hectares) and there he and Charity lived, first in a cabin and then in a two-storey, four-room log house as he cleared fields in pockets of fertile soil that produced good crops.

In 1885 Billing completed Blagdon Hill, his gracious home of simple design, using Haliburton granite for the structure and hand-hewn local oak for the window and door frames. In this isolated setting he planted an orchard, lilac bushes, locust trees, and cedars. With his home completed and his farm running well, Billing had time for active masonry. He built at least five stone houses and several brick ones for neighbours; possibly two were for Charity Billing's sisters, who visited and married into the Cooper and Sisson pioneer families still prominent in Haliburton County. Several of these buildings still stand. Billing also built one stucco house—Lakeview—that today overlooks Head Lake in Haliburton village.

Billing's most ambitious project was St. Peter's Anglican Church on Maple Lake. The first church, completed in 1887, was a frame, rough-cut structure. In 1901 the growing congregation celebrated the laying of the foundation stone of the second church. Billing designed, planned, and worked incessantly on the new building, which he completed in 1906. It was constructed by local workmen, entirely from local materials: stone from the adjacent hills, sand and gravel from the nearby Gull River, and pine timber cut and planed in a nearby mill. William Welch burned limestone into lime in a kiln at the edge of Maple Lake. Billing's perfectionism resulted in what Reynolds has described as "one of the loveliest churches in central Ontario." Today, deep in the land of rock and pines, travellers come upon this architectural gem which has stood for over a hundred years despite the rugged climate.

When Charity died in 1896, John intended to bury her at St. Peter's Church, but snowy weather prevented the trek down the hill. Instead the burial was at Blagdon Hill, where later he constructed a granite vault. John Billing died at age 85 in 1923, and was buried beside his wife. A generation later Napier Simpson lovingly preserved the Billing home, tools, books, and furnishings, adding to his own illustrious career as an expert in the restoration of old buildings. After his untimely death in 1978, Simpson was buried in the churchyard of John Henry Billing's St. Peter's Church. ■

33. A Workman in Seymour

Thomas F. McIlwraith

Fences are many things: barriers, boundary markers, occupiers of land, aesthetic delights. Some may be all of these. Here in Seymour stands a Workman fence, a style of tripods supporting thin poles or split rails. Workman fences are seen frequently between Lake Simcoe, Peterborough, and Kingston, but rarely elsewhere in Ontario. This style is a regional artifact, and it signals for the passer-by that this place is, quite possibly, in The Land Between.

Let me suggest a story, not much evident in this scene, but for which the facts are not in contradiction. In the 1840s, Seymour Township was laid out into Concessions—strips of land— from which hundred-acre (roughly forty hectares) farm lots were divided off. It was at that time

The Workman fence is among the best signals that one is in The Land Between. This one, near Stanwood, in Northumberland County, marks a boundary but is only a feeble barrier to passage. (photo courtesy of the author)

that a property line, currently expressed by this fence, was established between two iron bars sunk into the ground by the surveying crew. Chances are that no fence appeared for many years. Cutting a road, clearing a field, and putting up a house—all labour-intensive activities in a labour-scarce world—took priority. When a fence finally appeared, it surely was not this one. This structure would have been quite useless for the control of livestock in the age of mixed farming beginning in the 1860s and 1870s. By simply existing it defines a line, but the sharp change between grass and woods does the same thing, so it is (at least today) redundant as a boundary device. It does consume a wide swath, and that is how the earliest fence-builders in Ontario contended with a scarcity of labour and a surplus of land. It used local materials barely refined from being standing trees. Notice, finally, that the Workman fence stands on the land, and thus may easily be picked up and moved somewhere else. That suits the impermanent field patterns of the age of farm-making, when the size of plots within farms kept changing. In short, the Workman fence demonstrates common sense in the use of land and resources while providing reasonable definition of who owned what parcel in this part of Ontario.

Workman fences demonstrate the transition from natural materials to synthetic ones. They are successors to the snake-rail fence, which relied for stability on a dense overlapping of rails laid in a zig-zag fashion, reinforced by boulders or short stakes wedged in at the angles. Sometimes vertical stakes carried a wooden keeper across the top log to deter aggressive livestock from nosing the logs off the stack. The Workman tripod diminished that problem, but it could only stand if wired together. Hay-wire was the answer, increasingly available with the startup of the mixed farming economy, with its need for livestock feed. Hay also supplied urban horses, and plenty of short strands of wire, used for baling, found their way into the countryside.

For this Workman fence to be a barrier there would have to be one or two more rails per panel (the extent between tripods). Those rails are missing because they involve extra labour to install, each one being suspended in a wire sling from the crossing point. All indications are that this is a rebuilt Workman fence. Wire corrodes, rails fall down and, if no animals are to be controlled, those rails are not replaced. Labour costs are as much a consideration today as they were in the 19th century. The livestock farming that was once widespread in Seymour has faded, and huge tracts today stand idle and perhaps should never have been cleared in the first place. The young, homogeneous hardwood forest behind this fence shows what is happening repeatedly in The Land Between today. This Workman fence has evolved into a decoration, honouring a recognized tradition in The Land Between. ∎

34. A Castaway in The Land Between

Alan G. Brunger

The big, dark-brown block of granite is perched ominously by the side of the rapids between Buckhorn and Lower Buckhorn Lakes. Fully four metres in height and of similar breadth, it has stood there for at least 10,000 years, ever since it was transported to that point by an expanding ice-sheet and then dropped as the ice melted back at the end of the last Ice Age. North of Buckhorn big rocks are familiar objects in the Shield landscape; to the south, in the farming areas, they are hidden under moraine and till. However, in The Land Between, such as around Buckhorn, big rocks are somewhat of a novelty and tend to be given names by the locals, particularly when lodged in the backyard or on a roadside curve. All these displaced rocks—large or small—are referred to, correctly and scientifically, as glacially-transported erratics. They testify to the awesome power of the moving ice that once covered the area

Call it Balancing Rock or Council Rock. This massive pebble by the 19th century Buckhorn Inn is about four metres across. Thousands of years ago a glacier easily brought it here; today it is going nowhere.
(photo courtesy of author)

to a thickness of over a kilometre.

The Buckhorn erratic is known locally as Balancing Rock. Deep in the past it probably slid on to the ice surface, perhaps hundreds of kilometres away, and hitched a ride to its final precarious-looking resting place in front of the 19th-century Buckhorn Inn. Being of granite, it does not match in origin, age, mineral makeup—or even colour and texture—the sedimentary limestone stratum nearby. Such glacial debris is strewn throughout The Land Between, almost all of it in the form of mere pebbles that offer little contrast with the underlying bedrock. None are named, and are best recalled as nuisances in the vegetable gardens of local residents. But not Balancing Rock. Any chunk of granite that has been given a name must be exceptional, and massiveness provides justification. Balancing Rock clearly is named for its narrow base. Generations of revelers— members of rival lumber gangs fortified in the tavern at Buckhorn Inn more than a century ago, or teenagers today out for some fun on a summer weekend—have tried unsuccessfully to tip over this massive pebble.

And so it is not surprising that the Buckhorn erratic is also known by another name—Council Rock—commemorating what is believed to have been the practice by First Nations people of camping and conferring in its shelter. Oral tradition trumps documented evidence of this function. Perhaps Council Rock was where Ojibwa families gathered to organize seasonal cooperative hunting and fishing. Perhaps they discussed tribal law. Perhaps the Council of the Three Fires brought Ojibwa, Pottawatomi, and Ottawa peoples together by Council Rock to discuss matters in a spirit of cooperation, compromise, and consensus. It takes imagination to picture unrecorded scenes, but the accessibility of the Buckhorn Rapids site is a plausible rendezvous, one with ample sustenance during the prolonged time perhaps required for a large council.

We will never know how many erratics in The Land Between have acquired names. Probably there are hundreds, and each named stone adds interest to a local cultural landscape, and surely calls up an intriguing story. A single dramatic entity, The Rock at Buckhorn, stirs physiographic and cultural thoughts simultaneously. ■

Adam and Eve Rocks in Buckhorn.

35. Champlain in The Land Between

Dugald M. Carmichael & Brian S. Osborne

In late July of 1615, two heavily laden birchbark canoes sped southwards along the granite shoreline of La Mer Douce (Georgian Bay). The paddlers were ten Wendat (Hurons), Samuel Champlain, and two other Frenchmen. Preceded along this coast by ten well-armed French soldiers under his command, Champlain was aiming to "assist" some 2,500 Wendat and Algonquin warriors in an invasion of Iroquois territory south of Lake Ontario. Champlain's first commentary on The Land Between is a fish-story! "I named it The Freshwater Sea. It abounds … in trout, which are of enormous size … as much as four and a half feet long…. Also pike of like size, and a certain kind of sturgeon, a very large fish and marvellously good to eat."

The party reached Wendake (Huronia), homeland to about 30,000 Wendat, on August 1st. But the warriors were not yet ready for the warpath, so Champlain had time to visit a dozen villages on foot, recording in his journal that the whole region was "very fine, a well-cleared country where they plant much Indian corn, which comes up very well, as do squashes and sunflowers, from the seeds of which they make oil. There is abundance of vines and plums, raspberries, strawberries, small wild apples, butternuts and may-apples." On August 17th, Champlain was welcomed with jubilation and feasting at Cahiagué, a fortified settlement consisting of some 200 longhouses and 2,000 people.

By September 8th, all the warriors were assembled near Cahiagué and the campaign began. They paddled across Lake Simcoe, portaged overland to Balsam Lake, and then paddled downriver to the Bay of Quinte. Anyone who has travelled the Trent-Severn Waterway during Indian summer can well imagine Champlain's buoyant mood as the birchbark armada made its way, stopping often for up to 500 of the warriors to hunt deer by chasing them into the river. His commentary waxed poetic: "It is certain all this country is very fine and of pleasing character. Along the shores one would think the trees had been planted for ornament in most places. …Vines and butternut trees grow there in great quantity. The grapes come to maturity, but there remains always a very pungent acidity which one feels in the throat after eating many of them. This proceeds from a lack of cultivation." Clearly, Champlain was poised to become the Father not only of New France but also of Ontario viticulture!

By October 10th, the war-party had paddled down the Bay of Quinte, crossed Lake Ontario, cached their canoes, and attacked a fortified Onondaga village near today's Syracuse. They were repulsed and Iroquois arrows pierced Champlain's leg and knee. Unable to stand, he was carried back to the cached canoes in agony, "tied and bound on the back of one of our Indians." Breaking their promise to take him down the St. Lawrence to Quebec, his Wendat compan-

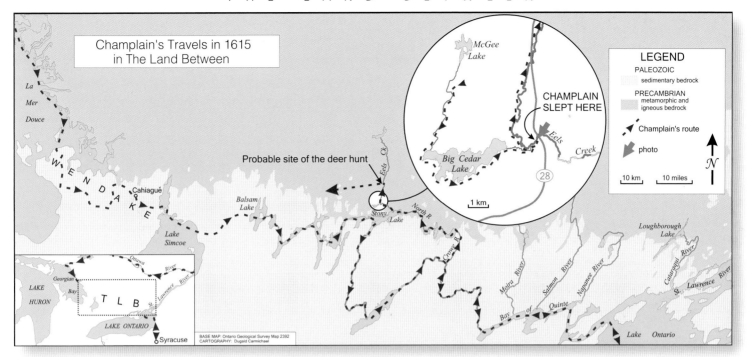

Champlain's Travels in 1615
in The Land Between

ions insisted that Champlain return to Cahiagué for the winter. We should be grateful, as, ill-prepared and wounded though he was, our explorer-cum-naturalist continued to observe and record his encounter with The Land Between.

After re-crossing Lake Ontario, they "entered a river some twelve leagues in length," from which they portaged half a league (between two and three kilometres) to a lake ten or twelve leagues in circumference where there were "swans, white cranes, bustards, ducks, teal, thrushes, larks, snipe, geese, and several other kinds of fowl too numerous to count." They paddled about ten leagues up another river and made camp on its bank. Here, they built wooden cabins chinked with moss, and a V-shaped fence of fir trees leading to an enclosure into which they would chase deer every second day.

During one such deer-hunt, Champlain, his wound largely healed, tracked a large red-headed bird (a pileated woodpecker?) and got lost in the bush without his compass.

For two rainy, sunless days he wandered back and forth. He shot a few birds to eat, and he prayed for courage to bear his misfortune, "should I have to remain abandoned in these wilds." On the third day, our intrepid explorer followed a small creek in the hope it would connect with the river he was seeking. The creek led to a lake about a league and a half in circumference, and Champlain followed its shoreline. Some distance down its outlet creek, he heard the sound of a waterfall. Soon he arrived at a clearing "where there were a great number of wild beasts" and also the junction of the creek with a river, "broad and wide." Imagine Champlain's joyous relief as he recognized a familiar portage-trail around the waterfall! Again, he slept in the open. The following day, "at my leisure," he proceeded upriver to where he knew the hunt-camp was located.

There has been much speculation as to where these events took place. To our knowledge, all such speculation has focussed variously on the Cataraqui, the Napanee, the

Salmon, or the Moira rivers. But none of these watersheds provides a credible match to the wealth of geographic detail in Champlain's narrative, and none of the implied routes is plausible from a paddler's perspective. Accordingly, we postulate that Champlain's Wendat companions took a much easier route home, via the Crowe River and its western tributary the North River. Stony Lake is the right size to be the lake of many birds, and this fact points to Eels Creek as the likely venue of the deer-hunt.

West of Eels Creek, near Big Cedar Lake, is an area that dovetails dramatically with Champlain's vivid account of getting lost in the bush. The image shows a waterfall just west of the Highway 28 bridge over Eels Creek. Just as Champlain described, this waterfall is clearly audible some distance upstream from where the creek from Big Cedar Lake empties into a quiet stretch of Eels Creek that cuts through a flat sandy terrace. Surely, this must be the place where Samuel Champlain slept on the ground some four centuries ago, confident that on the morrow he would easily rejoin his Wendat companions. ■

Looking up Eels Creek from the Highway 28 bridge on a rainy October day, 394 years after Champlain slept here. The mouth of the creek from Big Cedar Lake is 250 metres upriver from the waterfall. (photo courtesy of Dugald M. Carmichael)

36. Equivocal Archiving

Elwood H. Jones

When Peter Robinson led Irish settlers into The Land Between in 1825, leaders and followers kept records. Settler memories have reached us by song and dance passed down the generations, in memoirs and family histories, and in land records. Robinson kept administrative records which his nephew, John Beverley Robinson, donated to the Peterborough Public Library in 1895. A half century later the Library board decided that they were not running an archive and sent the Peter Robinson papers to the Provincial Archives of Ontario in Toronto. After 1967, when Peterborough finally had a museum, its new director retrieved them. The papers remain there, a local treasure, having survived despite the odds. Documents more bulky or deemed less important simply disappeared. Following the Peterborough flood of July 2004, many other records went to landfills. Zealous cleaners, cottage culture, and human carelessness added to the toll.

Equivocation persisted. Important local materials went to national and provincial repositories, among them those of Sandford Fleming, the Midland Railway, Catharine Parr Traill, Susanna Moodie, the Rice Lake Canoe Company, and Peterborough MP Bill Domm. On

The ornate post office window at Woodview, north of Stony Lake. (photo courtesy of Alan G. Brunger)

the other hand, records long held in Ottawa and Cornwall have returned, housed in the regional offices of Parks Canada in Peterborough. Howard Pammett, a prominent local historian, advised the Boyd family (of timber industry fame) to send many of their materials to the Public Archives of Canada. Other family papers later went to the Trent University Archives, created under the initiative of another local historian Edwin Guillet. He had alerted T. H. B. Symons, Trent's founding president, of the importance of retrieving early 19th-century court and governance records of the District of Newcastle pertaining to The Land Between. The Boyd family fonds are a further feather in Trent's cap.

Archival infrastructure in The Land Between is characterized by small or shared buildings. Consequently, there are few collections, chronic underfunding, inadequate staffing, and reliance on volunteers. Nothing is convenient for researchers. Modest museum archives developed at Lang Pioneer Village, the Centennial Museum, and at Hutchison House in Peterborough in 1975, but they mainly serve museum objectives. Trent University Archives, responsible for collecting First Nations and east central Ontario materials, gives priority to its university mandate. It is the best archives in The Land Between, but also has limited space and outreach.

The very active Trent Valley Archives (TVA), founded in 1988, is owned and operated by its members. Initially it sought to preserve private collections, often the meticulously organized family histories that universities and museums too often disdainfully dismissed. Today TVA is busy capturing the experience of people who left a mark in The Land Between; it publishes widely and shares history with street theatre and walks. Its quarterly magazine, *Heritage Gazette*, has no parallel in Ontario. Members believe that archives in The Land Between will be best established at the county level in institutions meeting international standards and offering extensive, and committed, community outreach. Excellent models in Simcoe and Wellington counties, beyond The Land Between, show what might so easily be accomplished.

Amid the indecision about who should tend to what, history falls through the cracks. Peterborough, for example, once was one of Canada's major industrial towns, yet today few significant collections of local industrial, labour, or business materials exist. Less would be lost if the public were more sensitive to what is worth saving and if proper, well-managed and respected places stood ready to receive documents and photographs. Yet at present, as each year passes, the stories of The Land Between become, sadly, harder and harder to read and share among ourselves and with our descendants. Reader, check your attic and talk to local politicians, and perhaps you can help stem the erosion of our documentary heritage. ∎

37. Of the Place, for the Place: Swirls in Space and Time

James Raffan

Most mornings, I greet the day with dogs and an early jaunt on Cranberry Lake. In winter, it's skates, snowshoes, or rubber boots. In summer, we head out by canoe, often across the lake, to a place where a granite cliff rises out of the water, not far from where a family of loons have nested since my wife and I moved to this corner of eastern Ontario.

When the water is calm, the canoe slides silently into two worlds simultaneously. There is the physicality of rock and water. In reflection is the silvery mix of rock, sky, and dreams. Often I imagine a human face in the shadowed patterns on that cliff. That mirrored countenance conjures images of First Nation people who might have stood on this outcropping long ago, looking out the other way—except that before 1832 this manufactured lake was

a creek flowing down to Cataraqui Bay. In stillness, or when snowflakes fall silently on black December water, the canoe bends perception, like the swirls of a paddle in time and space.

As a first-generation Canadian, my boyhood heart was captured by the blue lake and rocky shores of Haliburton and Algonquin Park where the smell of pine, the sound of loon calls, and the feel of cool water on sun-warmed skin became part of a sense of place that was rooted in the Canadian Shield. Recollections of paddling, first for day outings, then overnights, and eventually multi-day canoe trips occupied—and continue to occupy—more classroom, lecture hall, and inter-office musings in the offseason than I'd care to admit.

But like many an immigrant's child, the romance of adventure was not the stuff of solid career foundations, so my head decreed (voiced in my mother's often unintelligible Aberwegian doric) that I had best get an education and seek employment that would make a more substantial contribution to humanity than puddling around in canoes might deliver.

By luck or serendipity, my wife and I landed teaching jobs in eastern Ontario and settled here on Cranberry Lake, north of Kingston, in the proverbial "best of both worlds." Here, a short paddle can take you from old field and limestone to forest grasping the geological interminglings of much older rocks from the immutable Canadian Shield. Boat traffic fills the Rideau waterway for much of the year, water levels are carefully controlled, and yet the essential character of the land prevails.

The genius of this place is its betweenness. Within minutes of all the easy amenities of lowland commerce in the Quebec-Windsor corridor we can lie in bed and listen to loons, often in prelude to coyotes who take their place on the ridge in the wee hours and sing their way into our sleeping consciousness. And the vessel that connects us physically, and psychically, to this threshold place is the canoe. It's not lowland here. It's not Shield here. It's The Land Between, a little of both, and the canoe—a vessel of the place and *for* the place—moves effortlessly from one to the other. ∎

38. Stump Fences and Ghost Farms

Ron Reid

Aragged line of upended pine stumps along a naked ridge of granite marks a brief passage of human enterprise in a difficult landscape. Behind this primitive fence, second-growth forest now stretches unbroken for kilometres, but these bleached roots show that settlers a century ago had dreams of farmland on this rugged terrain.

Settlement roads and land grants lured newcomers into The Land Between. The familiar pattern of rectangular 100-acre (approximately 40 hectares) lots, neatly laid out with nary a thought to the natural lines of the landscape, must have conveyed

"Lot 29, Concession VIII, Dalton Township" sounds like the address of any one of thousands of active farm sites throughout rural Ontario. This particular lot 29, however, is a sad spot, where a would-be farming family failed, leaving only picturesque fragments to mark their trials in The Land Between. (photo courtesy of the author)

mental images of the rich agricultural lands to the south. From the scale of the ancient stumps captured in this fence, the virgin timber had to be sizeable, further strengthening the promise of fertile ground.

How long then would it take, after the back-breaking labour of clearing the land was complete, before the bitter realization of the land's real potential set in? Stripped of tree cover that had taken centuries to gain a foothold, the smooth humps of bedrock soon began to show through. Even in the pockets of deeper soil, the acidic sands proved a poor base for crops, and most markets for the sale of farm products were distant.

The weathered rows of stumps testify that this farm had a few cattle suitable for rough grazing, likely a mix of shorthorns and other hardy breeds. On the former fields nearby ancient piles of stones speak to desperate attempts to improve the land for row crops. A log barn and wooden shanty likely completed the pastoral setting, but all trace of these structures is long gone.

For a brief period these marginal farms were able to scrape by supplying fresh pork, peas, and barley to lumber camps in the vicinity. Often the men of the farm would spend their winters in those same camps, harvesting the white pine and hauling the logs to the Black River in readiness for the spring freshet that would float them to the mill.

But soon the big pine was gone, the local markets for the farm were gone, and much of the soil that formed a thin mantle over the bedrock was gone too. Most of the hardscrabble farms were left to nature, often cleared and abandoned within a single generation. Families moved to the vast beckoning expanse of the Canadian West, or retreated to the growing cities.

Here and there, in places such as Sadowa just to the east of this farm, pockets of better soil allowed farming to be sustained, and tight-knit families put down roots in their communities. But for much of The Land Between all that remains of that brief burst of short-lived promise are silent fences of stumps and stone, lost in a landscape returning to the bush. Just as many of the villages of that era are now ghost towns, only the ghosts of those early farms remain. ■

39. Earthworms: Exotic Newcomers to The Land Between

Tara Sackett

Earthworms are not native to The Land Between, or even to Ontario. From the end of the last glaciation, nearly ten thousand years ago, to the arrival of the Europeans, the invertebrate fauna in our soils was restricted to smaller creatures, visible only with a microscope or sharp and searching eyes.

The seventeen species of terrestrial earthworms, or *oligochaeta*, in Ontario

Dendrobaena octaedra *makes its unhurried way along a gravel country road in The Land Between.*
(photo courtesy of the author)

are all of European origin. Like many exotic species, they came to North America as hitchhikers in soils and sundries brought by the Europeans to begin their lives on this continent. The first published record of earthworms in Ontario appears to be from 1874 by Gustav Eisen, a Swedish immigrant to the United States and a remarkable biologist, who found several species of worms in the Niagara peninsula. Their earliest movement north would have occurred in the decades that followed. Some worms will have reached The Land Between with the settlers establishing farms in the pockets of arable land (or the failed attempts in the broader fabric of non-arable land). Other worms, such as the large, wriggly nightcrawler (*Lumbricus terrestris*), will have accompanied the increasing numbers of cottagers and holidayers bent on catching the plentiful fish. Many used the Victoria Railway, completed north from Lindsay, through Fenelon Falls and Kinmount, to Haliburton during the 1870s. Today The Land Between is dotted with communities of worms, thriving often beside settlements and boat landings where genesis and renewal of the populations comes from tossing the bait out of the bucket at the end of the day.

Some of the species of worms found in The Land Between will have started arriving during the 1920s, when the automobile began to make its mark across the landscape. These smaller worms are not carried intentionally but, instead, are able to use the roadside as habitat and passageway. On gravelled roads, these species live in the mounds of soil and organic matter to the side, and are probably carried farther along the corridor with each passage of the grader's blade.

Earthworms are appropriately renowned for their beneficial activities in agricultural land, yet the same behaviours that enrich our garden soils may be detrimental to forest soils in The Land Between. Earthworms rapidly consume the leaves that blanket the forest floor, and churn the soils that had gradually formed their profiles over hundreds or thousands of years. The pace of decomposition, previously set by the microflora and tiny fauna native to Ontario soils, has been dramatically accelerated.

The future of a forest lies in the layers formed by the fallen leaves of years before. In these horizons seeds germinate, microflora release nutrients, and fine roots begin to grow. When these soil horizons disappear, the dynamics of plant regeneration and cycling of carbon and nutrients change.

Our team of researchers at the University of Toronto are working with Haliburton Forest and Wildlife Reserve to try and understand what these changes will mean to the sustainability of these forests. So far, worms, like many invasive species, have not spread as widely through this area as in southern Ontario. But exotics—even humble worms—travel easily, and careful watchfulness for non-native wildlife may be important for The Land Between. ■

40. The American Eel: "This Manna that Nourishes Us"

Robert B. MacGregor

Did you know that virtually all the eels in The Land Between (and other Ontario waters) are female? Were you aware that the life cycle of this species—the American Eel (*Anguilla rostrata*)—begins in the Sargasso Sea, far out in the Atlantic Ocean? Once male and female eels reach the estuaries of eastern North America, their paths diverge. The females head inland to the nutritious waters of such places as

The Land Between, where they spend some twelve to fifteen years feeding and fattening up, and then leave to rendezvous with the males in the ocean. Returning to the Sargasso, the eels breed and spawn, and then die. The Land Between is just one, albeit lengthy, stop in an elaborate life cycle covering thousands of kilometres.

Ichthyologists have long recognized that the eel fisheries of the lower St. Lawrence River, towards

This large female eel was captured in September 2009 in Mississippi Lake, near Perth, in the Ottawa River system. Eels of this size were almost unknown in The Land Between by this date. (photo courtesy of Eric Robertson, OMNR)

Rivière du Loup, are among the most productive in the world. Those large, fecund females from Ontario's inland waters have had a lot to do with it. Some penetrated as far as Lake Timiskaming, Lake Opeongo and the headwaters of the many tributaries of the Ottawa River system; others reached Mazinaw Lake, the Kawarthas, and the extensive waters of The Land Between. The Jesuit missionary Paul le Jeune wrote from Quebec in 1634: "It is wonderful how many of these fish are found in this great river [the St. Lawrence]," adding, "it is thought that this great abundance [of eels] is supplied by some lakes in the country farther north, which, discharging their waters here, make us a present of this manna that nourishes us ..." These could well have been the words of First Nations people, stewards of this rich resource for thousands of years. Eels were an important food for them, and, in addition, eel skins were used to fashion bow grips and treat rheumatic joints. One wonders whether Samuel de Champlain, having explored through The Land Between not long before Père le Jeune wrote, was aware of the migratory connection contemplated.

The life cycle of the American Eel is fraught with danger at the best of times, but the risk has been seriously exacerbated by modern conditions. Contaminants and pollutants have affected fertility and survival, as have invasive species and diseases. The parasitic bladder worm from Europe is just one instance. Migrating fish are killed by hydroelectric turbines or have their passage obstructed by locks and dams. At least fourteen hydroelectric installations complicate passage through the Trent River, an important access route to The Land Between. The decline has been almost imperceptible over the past century, partly because eels fell out of favour in Ontario as a diet or sport fish of interest, and record-keeping has been wholly inadequate.

Eels have been overfished intensively at all continental life stages across North America. They were being taken primarily for export, and the sustainability of the total North American harvest is now in doubt. In the early 1980s, eels constituted half the value of all commercial fish-landings from Lake Ontario. As juveniles entering that lake, some would have travelled onward into The Land Between, and as adults would have attempted to return to Sargasso Sea via Lake Ontario, forming part of that harvest. A few eels still do, but by the start of the 21st century, numbers had fallen precipitously, to barely one per cent of the 1980s level. In response to a provincial government initiative, Ontario's commercial eel fishery was closed in 2004, and the recreational one a year later. Still, by 2010 the species was approaching extirpation—total destruction—and it has been placed on Ontario's list of endangered species. That is rather timid language for an approaching collapse of a species, once widely abundant, that holds special economic, cultural, and natural heritage significance.

The Ontario part of the eel life story is bleak, and clearly the entire cycle is in trouble. For those thinking about the ecology of The Land Between, a great concern is biodiversity. The female American Eel makes a unique contribution to diversity, yet in the second decade of the 21st century she is so rarely seen in the inland waters as to defy routine assessment. Recovery of healthy numbers in The Land Between is proving to be a slow, daunting process that will extend over several generations of eels, reaching well into the 22nd century. Now that the commercial fishery is closed, hydroelectric facilities are by far the largest single threat to the survival and recovery of the American Eel. And herein lies the conundrum. Hydro-electricity can be an environmentally sound product if its collateral damages are alleviated; recovery of species at risk and biodiversity are likewise laudable goals. However, careless generation of electricity from waterpower comes at the price of damaging the life cycle of the American Eel and other native migratory species. If we do not construct and operate these power facilities carefully, we threaten that coveted biodiversity in The Land Between and elsewhere.

Resolving this dilemma is today's challenge, neglected heretofore, and each of us in Ontario has a responsibility to address it now and in the years to come. In 2013 we have the knowledge and ability to do much better than make simplistic trade-offs of one renewable resource for another. As many more power generation facilities are planned, we need to be careful that mistakes of the past are corrected, not repeated. ■

41. Kinmount: Hub on the Fringe

Guy Scott

The edge of the Canadian Shield slashes its way across The Land Between like a jagged piece of broken glass. Granite and limestone collide; cascading rapids and waterfalls punctuate river systems. Such is The Land Between, historically often better suited for moving logs (and maybe canoes) than land-based human beings.

Settlement ran into that unruly edge as early as the 1820s. And, there, the advancing frontier stalled for a generation. Breaking into, and perhaps even through, the edge was a goal of the Provincial colonization road

The Austin Sawmill and, beyond the dam, the restored railway station: at the hub, in the forest.
(photo courtesy of the author)

program of the 1850s, intended to encourage and assist farming settlement in a rugged terrain. One of a half-dozen prongs poking northward from the older farmlands was the Bobcaygeon Road, aimed from Pigeon Lake towards Lake Nipissing. Barely one-eighth of the way its route simultaneously crossed the Monck Road (a military trace between Orillia and the Ottawa Valley), Burnt River, and the edge of the Shield. Convergence of three arteries, a bridge, and a change in landforms cries out for a village, and here the hamlet of Kinmount sprang into existence, a sudden hub in The Land Between. To river and road add rail in the 1870s. The Victoria Railway saw Kinmount as a worthy stop along its illusory path towards the upper Ottawa River. In the following decade the Irondale, Bancroft and Ottawa Railway, a grandly-named misadventure, chose Kinmount as the terminus for its line branching off through the woods north of town. The Hub, indeed!

Each spring, logs driven down the Burnt River bumped and jostled past the falls at Kinmount on their way to sawmills along the Kawartha Lakes. But when the Victoria Railway reached town, as many as eight sawmills promptly went up. Logs once destined onward now were hauled out, sawn into lumber, and loaded onto railroad cars headed southward through Lindsay to outside markets, primarily in the United States. Iron ore mined in the area was shipped through Kinmount too, and there were even a few farmers for whom it was their market town. Manufactured goods destined for Haliburton County funnelled through Kinmount; hunters, anglers, cottagers, and tourists stocked up there. Merchants prospered and grand stores lined the Bobcaygeon Road. Other would-be Kinmounts languished, but The Hub, the gateway, bustled.

Despite—or perhaps because of—the diversity of The Land Between, living on the fringe was risky business. Farming was rarely viable—a pocket of alluvium here, a pasture there—and faded, often within a generation or two. Lumbering had declined by the 1920s as the seemingly limitless forests were cut-over and the best timber harvested. By the 1960s all Kinmount sawmills were closed. Beginning in the 1930s, construction of hard-surfaced roads and commitment to snow plowing in winter catered to car and truck. Traffic became dispersed over a network of country roads, reflecting a thoroughly mobile society; the railway was doomed.

Kinmount was still The Hub, however, persisting stoically in place even as its context was being utterly transformed. Municipal officials have deftly used that advantage to create a new prosperity based on auto-oriented tourism and cottaging along Burnt River and lakes in the vicinity. Employers visualize the annual cycle along modern lines: summer and the rest of the year. Burnt River, long since bereft of logs, has become a canoe route. The Victoria Railway roadbed is a year-round recreational corridor for hikers, cyclists, snowmobilers, and quad riders. The restored Austin Sawmill Museum recalls the forestry era. A movie theatre has been featuring favourite oldies on summer weekends. Artisans have set up shops in the community centre. Retired folk may be content to do little more than absorb the natural beauty of the area. In Kinmount, The Land Between assumes a gentle, somewhat refined wilderness quality, lying between the boring farmlands southward and the deep, almost impenetrable forests of a truly rugged northland. ■

42. On the Road to Lakehurst Cheese

Alan G. Brunger

On the southern peninsula of Harvey Township, inland from Pigeon Lake, lies the hamlet of Lakehurst. There, opposite the former general store and post office, stood, until its recent removal, the old cheese factory. Inside, for many years, there remained a horse-drawn milk cart, a relic from the decades before 1960.

Each day it would ply up and down the concession lines, stopping at each roadside milk stand to pick up the forty-gallon metal churns that were waiting after the morning milking was over. Dairy cows never stop giving, and so in all kinds of weather—winter chill or summer heat—the Lakehurst driver could be seen manhandling the churns across

B. EASON GEN. STORE
LAKEHURST, ONT.

Lakehurst, a quintessential Ontario crossroads hamlet, here viewed towards the west in the 1940s. The cheese factory is the long building in the centre, behind the two-storey house. Eason's store stands across the road. (photo courtesy of The Greater Harvey Historical Society)

141

the narrow gap between stand and cart, securing each with long metal pins inserted through the handles to one of the three vertical posts along the middle of the cart. This was the only precaution taken to deal with whatever rough surfaces might be encountered on the return journey to the cheese factory. As late as the 1950s many roads continued to be of earth, unsurfaced, and filled each spring and fall with water and chuckholes. One wonders how effective the cart's special springing was under such challenges.

The Lakehurst cheese factory was typical of hundreds of such establishments that emerged in Ontario late in the 19th century. Those in The Land Between represented the northward expansion of this farm-based enterprise in Ontario. Milk, from cattle that had been traditionally part of mixed farming, was being processed in The Land Between for export as cream or butter and, in particular, as cheese.

Milk delivered at the Lakehurst factory was first tested for butterfat prior to separation of the cream; both cream and milk were usually destined for markets in local towns. Production of butter from the whey followed and, finally, manufacture of the cheese. The latter could profitably be exported to distant markets in the pre-refrigeration period.

Improvement to land transportation greatly increased the exporting capability of the farms in The Land Between. Although far from perfect, railways offered a much smoother ride than did passage along rural roads, allowing fluid milk to travel unimagined distances and remain fresh. Tiny spur lines probed the edges of The Land Between, and, for more than half a century, the milk car became a recognized component of the local mixed train, running along lightweight tracks to places like Coboconk, Kinmount, Bobcaygeon, Lakefield, Bonarlaw, Tamworth, Yarker and

Lakehurst cheese factory, southwest corner of lot 9, concession 13, Harvey Township. Sketch by Olli Virkamaki.
(courtesy of the Greater Harvey Historical Society)

Lakehurst in 1915 with the old community hall (right) and cheese factory (left), and a young family strolling by the up-to-date telephone line. Photographer unknown.(courtesy of the Greater Harvey Historical Society)

Harrowsmith. Such railroad activity faded everywhere as highway transport took hold, using the network of paved and well-gravelled roads, reaching all areas after World War II, to carry milk and butter, and cheese too.

Cheese-making is such a fine story for The Land Between, a small-town industry supported by a veneer of pastoral farming stretching along the northerly edge of true agricultural Ontario. Cattle could graze selectively on the thin and stony soils that repelled machinery designed for big rectangular fields. The Lakehurst cheese factory was but one of several such enterprises in the Harvey Township area;

others were at Buckhorn and Cedardale. As more efficient cheese operations extended their spheres of influence, they smothered the little operators once so central to villages in The Land Between. Lakehurst fell silent and the milk cart was put away, forever. And by 2008 the building itself had vanished: loading stage, machinery, cart and all.

Further afield the small-town cheese tradition lives on. Names like Wilton and Balderson come to mind. This is cheese for the 21st century from The Land Between, a product that is attracting national, even international, attention. ∎

43. Pictograph Meets Petroglyph on Mazinaw Lake

John Wadland

The Land Between is home to a number of provincial parks, but none is more emblematic of the complexities of the mosaic ecotone than Bon Echo, located in the Addington Highlands, north of Napanee. Written into its dramatic geology, bountiful forests, and beautiful lakes is a human story that dates from time immemorial. Steep rock faces displaying over 250 pictographs rise 100 metres from the clear, deep waters of Mazinaw Lake, remembering Algonquins who passed this way thousands of years before the arrival of Europeans. These people were dislodged from neighbouring traditional lands in the colonial period, and their descendants—for example, the Ardoch Algonquin First Nation—remain locked in legal battles to defend their Aboriginal rights from the rapacious resourcism engulfing them to this day. Extraction began in 1854 with the construction of the Addington colonization road, now recognized as Highway 41. Nineteenth-century lumber barons and miners depended on produce from the 100-acre (about 40 hectares) farms free-granted along the

The face of Bon Echo (photo courtesy Alan G. Brunger)

roadway to feed their labourers. Once the forests had been logged out, and the mines abandoned, farming too disappeared, leaving behind a scarred barren. What today appears in much of the region to be a pristine wilderness is really a naturally recovering industrial landscape requiring educated eyes for reading its stories.

This "pristine wilderness" likely would not exist at all were it not for the 1959 gift to the Province of Ontario of the original Bon Echo site by Merrill Denison, the successful Canadian playwright and radio dramatist who is also remembered for his corporate histories of Massey-Harris, Molson's, Ontario Hydro, and the Bank of Montreal. His mother—theosophist, feminist, journalist, and successful businesswoman, Flora MacDonald Denison—had grown up in a logger's shanty on the Skootamatta River, near Actinolite. In 1910 she and her American husband, Howard Denison, purchased the Bon Echo Inn and surrounding acreage from its original builder, converting it to a retreat for artists and writers and centering its intellectual mission on the democratic ideals of the American poet Walt Whitman. The inn was positioned on a beach near the narrows of Mazinaw Lake, opposite the massive rock face carrying the Algonquin pictographs. As testament to her mission, Flora hired two stonemasons from Aberdeen, Scotland, to cut into the Bon Echo Rock in foot-high letters a fragment from Whitman's poem, "Song of Myself." Headed "Old Walt," it reads:

> *My foothold is tenon'd and mortised in granite*
> *I laugh at what you call dissolution*
> *And I know the amplitude of time*

These words seem, somehow, a more fitting reminder of the original inhabitants of Massanoga, the Algonkian name believed to have been used to refer to the rock, and meaning "it is painted" or variations on that phrase. Perhaps recognition of a possible relationship was intended. Irrespective of intent, ancient pictograph and this modern petroglyph share the same canvas.

Merrill Denison inherited the Bon Echo site following Flora's death in 1921. He continued to operate the inn in the spirit enshrined by his mother until the arrival of the Great Depression, when it failed. Before the inn and many of its adjacent outbuildings tragically burned to the ground in 1936, the Denison family had hosted some of Canada's best-remembered visual artists. F. M. Bell-Smith, Arthur Lismer, Franz Johnston, C. W. Jefferys, J. W. Beatty, Franklin Carmichael, A. J. Casson, Dorothy Stevens, Charles Comfort and others all have left their witness to the place in landscape images now populating public and private collections across the country.

Following the fire, Merrill summered at his undamaged cabin, "Greystones," which he used as a retreat for writing even after donating the site to the province. In 1955, on the occasion of the 100th anniversary of the publication of Whitman's *Leaves of Grass*, he re-dedicated Old Walt in a formal ceremony for the Canadian Authors' Association. Merrill's best-known plays, including *Marsh Hay, Brothers in Arms, The Weather Breeder,* and *From Their Own Place,* illustrate—sometimes comically, sometimes sadly—the colourful lives of the backwoods people, his neighbours in the immediate region.

Bon Echo Provincial Park, now amounting to 66 square kilometres and still firmly anchored by the big rock, was not formally opened to the public until 1965, ten years before the death of Merrill Denison. In 1976 the Canadian Conservation Institute in Ottawa began the formal study and recording of the Mazinaw Lake pictographs. ∎

44. Underutilization— or Overexpectation?

Thomas F. McIlwraith

What might first be construed as abandonment is more properly to be viewed simply as changing land use. Land and facilities rise and fall in the degree of intensity of use. Here, in Seymour, is a scene of underutilization—or perhaps of the consequences of overexpectation.

The roadway with the closed, slightly battered gate receives occasional use, but could probably grow back green again without further attention. It is of the era before truckloads of gravel, or tar, or asphalt, those substances that only slowly biodegrade, marking their place long after active roles have ceased. This right-of-way is of the age of horses, wagons, and sleighs, when one simply drove through and made ruts and left a green strip down the middle. In pre-automobile days farm lanes and country roads blended together visibly as one, without precedence. The hierarchy of main roads and secondary roads spread only so far from the bigger centres into the extremities of the countryside, petering out altogether in places like this.

As our roadway dropped out of regular, or even infrequent use, it blended back into the terrain. In this case, that point is reached less than halfway to the barn. At one time it continued on back to a small house, the site apparently marked by a thin line of stones directly in front of the gambrel end of the barn. Or that is where a house should be, when one looks at a hundred farmsteads around the province and acknowledges standard patterns that are freely and unconsciously repeated. Between that place and the barn stands the yard, upon which faced the "back" door of the house. Any door on the side facing the road—what most people would call the front—would be principally for ceremony, or perhaps just mere decoration. Watch for them covered with plastic sheeting for insulation in the winter, and the idea of these apparent entrances not being for use will strike home.

The board siding missing from the barn gives it that unused look too and is a focus for the palpable dereliction of this place. The battered gate—a 1940s artifact—and the eroded patch of gravel reinforce the image. The entire site has changed from a hive of rural enterprise and become a pasture, uniformly bland and green, where once a variety of domestic and farming functions would have given many hues and textures. Note how short and tidy the grass is; be patient for a few hours and the cattle will amble through.

This farmstead has become a farm field in an enterprise now centred elsewhere. The family that once lived here has become redundant and moved away to join the world of cities beyond, while those members too old to adapt have lingered, probably in a nearby village, and then died off. The exposure of gravel shows how very thin the soil is in Seymour, just where the good farmland of southern Ontario

runs out into the limestone plain and the Precambrian Shield beyond. After an effort at being a viable mixed agricultural enterprise, culminating in the raised gambrel-roofed barn of the first decade of the 20th century, this site has settled back to what it truly is: scrub land. The barn once served as a shelter and storage building, and perhaps still does, but only in a half-hearted sort of way. It is fully amortized (should anyone care to think in those terms) yet, with a sound foundation and a typically well-crafted framework, may stand up indefinitely, even as the boards flap and then blow away. They're just details.

As for the house, its parts—windows, doors, possibly even a brick veneer once laid up over board siding—long have entered the market among builders engaged in restoration or reproduction architecture. Brick chimney stacks were coveted by scavengers who cared not that water would get in and rot would inevitably follow. People buy up former farmhouses for animal shelters, or dismantle them and recycle the huge squared logs. Whatever its fate, the house we feel certain once stood here in Seymour has vanished, leaving barely a trace for the consideration of roadside philosophers. ∎

Pasturing cattle wander through the fading residue of the small family farm, once a vibrant centre of buildings, people, stock, and machinery. (photo courtesy of the author)

45. Deloro

Roy T. Bowles & Louise Livingstone

Deloro—the name—smacks of gold, although perhaps not for people unfamiliar with Romance languages or the chemists' Periodic Table of the Elements. But the secret was out, and the discovery of gold north of Madoc in 1866 stirred an early, though brief, gold rush into The Land Between. Gold here was mixed with arsenic and other minerals, however, and it took more than thirty years to establish a profitable separating process. Credit a Danish engineer (Peter Kirkegaard) and a Queen's University metallurgist (D. S. Kirkpatrick) with the invention. But gold operations were short-lived, ceasing in 1902 when the main mine flooded.

Deloro—the mine—was far from done, however. Arsenic, a by-product there since 1879, became of special interest in 1907. In that year an enterprise later called

Men line up to show off the substantial Deloro plant in the 1920s. (photo courtesy of Trent University Archives)

Deloro Smelting and Refining Company—DSRC—established a new industrial complex there involving silver ore from Cobalt, Ontario. That ore contained arsenic (plus cobalt and nickel) and became the subject of experimentation from which another Queen's metallurgist (H.T. Kalmus) developed a process for refining cobalt. Going one more step, an American inventor in the DSRC laboratory (Elwood Haynes) developed stellite, an alloy of cobalt, chromium, and tungsten that is hard, can withstand high temperature, and makes highly efficient cutting tools and munitions. In exchange for supplying cobalt, Haynes granted DSRC rights to produce stellite and distribute it in Europe and the British Commonwealth. Such a sequence of inventions underscores the character of The Land Between as a place of heightened diversity.

Deloro—the company town—had begun in the mining period, significantly expanded in the industrial era, and was incorporated in 1919. Demand for munitions and industrial products had been growing during World War I and, by 1917, DSRC had nearly 400 employees. During the interwar period DSRC started producing arsenic-based insecticides to fight boll weevil infestations in American cotton crops. The call for stellite for making aircraft and armaments increased dramatically during World War II, leading to the employment of some 300 workers. Ores from Africa, previously processed in Belgium, were redirected to Deloro and the plant was once again modified to handle them. One last transformation occurred in the 1950s, with federal funds used to establish Cold War defence programs. Demand for cobalt (some from Morocco) was sustained by the market for stellite used in making jet engine turbine blades and high-speed cutting tools. Post-war prosperity at Deloro was fleeting, however; the stellite and metals department moved to Belleville in 1955 and, in 1958, the Deloro processing plant closed.

Deloro—the abandoned site—was now an industrial brownfield, not what one commonly thinks of in The Land Between. When DSRC failed to comply with an order in 1978 to stop arsenic from seeping into the Moira River, the Ontario Ministry of the Environment (MOE) took control. After thirty years and a multimillion-dollar site management program, the hazardous wastes—arsenic, cobalt, copper, nickel, and low-level radioactive material—are coming under control. In 2012 MOE was still at work, placing clay covers over the waste, planting native vegetation, and preparing an interpretive heritage plan.

Deloro is an important industrial heritage site. Complex ores stimulated metallurgical inventiveness leading to products of sophisticated and strategic importance internationally. Deloro contributed to national industrial development and defense programs during both World Wars and the Korean War. DSRC provided jobs for new Canadians and for local people struggling to make inhospitable land produce. But apparent success must be balanced against the costs that working conditions in mine and mill imposed on the lives of workers, too often leading to premature deaths. Part of The Land Between had been severely degraded, and management of the site continues to be at huge public cost, now and long into the future. ∎

46. At Home in The Land Between

Leora Berman

When I sit quietly in my backyard overlooking one of the beautiful lakes of Haliburton, I am viscerally aware and appreciative of the landscape that envelops me. A relationship has formed with this land—The Land Between—that has grown gradually over the past few years. It is comprised of knowledge put together, piece by piece, and now wholly integrated, even though I occupy only a small space and time within it.

Haliburton is in the middle of this geography. The rock and water here are typical of what extends across the terrain in all directions. I can walk less than one kilometre from any point in the landscape and reach water—a small wetland, a lake, river or stream. I can bask on sun-soaked rock barrens along with the butterflies and nighthawks. After returning from a journey to the southern Great Lakes, I know I am home. In The Land Between I can look up into the clear night, and see the Milky Way—innumerable stars sparkling, signalling and welcoming me. A loon's cry across the still night air and over the low dense hills tells me that I have arrived. In the morning and throughout the day I have many

A dock in a rippling lake is a special place for reflecting on The Land Between. (photo courtesy of the author)

visitors; the land is dancing with wildlife. Species from across the province congregate here: frogs, birds, reptiles. The families of both the crow and the raven extend into this habitat and their calls compete for attention; the ruby-throated hummingbird controls local air space. This is the meeting place of the moose and the deer who together haunt the forests. This land is occupied, as well, by those that prefer it to all other places—the slippery five-lined skink whose quick flicker can jolt a day-dreamer by a shore, those contented turtles meandering over ancestral and invisible trails, and the whip-poor-will that intones lullabies outside the window each evening. And the unseen permeates the space too: the echoes of the Anishinabek and Algonquin whose stories are whispered in the paths and shadows, and along the waterways. Their presence may be felt through the songs of the animals that resound in Ojibwa, or in the shapes of the forests and trees.

I am one of the new settlers, joining a long line of vigorous innovators and choosing this harsh and remote place as a home. I move rocks to make way for a small garden, and travel long distances to reach markets and friends. I clad my character through braving dark and isolative winters, to release in carefree summer play surrounded by children's laughter and the snaps and zings of miniature winged insects. The hum of a distant outboard motorboat carrying my neighbour on a daybreak trolling adventure arouses me gently; I find it surprisingly unobtrusive, despite its suggestion of everything industrial. I am privileged to be able to join historic and prehistoric walkabouts in this setting.

I am a part of The Land Between, as it is part of me. It surrounds me at the same time as it infuses me with its essence, communicating and conveying in a dance with my cells and my spirit. In these quiet moments I feel an animate tension between utter yearning and perpetual joy—the reflection of my friendship with this land, My Home. ■

Afterword

Daphne Alley

As I write, I look back on the over ten years since Peter Alley began his voyage of research and discovery of the part of Ontario which has come to be known as The Land Between. It is strange indeed that no one had identified it as a landscape, unique and precious, before this. There was a reason. In their efforts to make people aware of the environment, early scientists chose to focus on specific places which were discrete and entire, bearing little visible relationship to the adjacent land or to each other. Many

of these examples were protected in publicly-held conservation reserves. Even when it became common knowledge that habitats for wildlife depended on contiguous stretches of land, both to allow for travel and to reduce the impact of human activity, the search for significant pockets of land continued.

It is ironic that Peter began his quest merely to enlarge one such conservation reserve. Ever curious, his endless questioning produced, however, more questions than answers. At one university, one scholar acknowledged that this land was an ecotone and, yes, it did encompass a swath of territory stretching basically east and west. But that silo of knowledge did not make useful connection with others, which irritated Peter, and gradually he discovered links in more and more interesting ways. Horticultural zones followed The Land Between, as did geological zones, watersheds and, today, recreational areas. Settlement roads, projected before Confederation in 1867, were defined by the curious pockets of tillable soil in The Land Between. In local areas Peter met individuals with deep knowledge

of particular landforms. Some always knew the land was different—and special—but could not explain how or why until it was put into the context of The Land Between.

The more Peter learned about The Land Between, the more he became concerned about the pressures on the land by the changing population patterns. Development posed a very real threat. The Land Between, with its thin soil and porous limestone, is extremely vulnerable to contamination, and once defiled, almost certainly beyond repair. This concern changed Peter from an interested researcher into a passionate advocate.

And now in The Land Between we are fortunate in having some wonderful reflections on the land from perspectives even broader than Peter may ever have imagined. One of his last activities—and such an enjoyable one—was recruiting knowledgeable, thinking people from different fields of the environment movement and persuading them to write about The Land Between. One of his great accomplishments was recruiting Thomas McIlwraith, a gifted writer, who took on the editorship of this book.

A Selection of Related Reading on The Land Between

Alan G. Brunger

Few publications come close to describing The Land Between in its entirety and, as a subject, it falls between stools in a literary sense. As a designation "The Land Between" cuts across just about any conceivable thematic or spatial boundary. Furthermore, this expression has been used, quite appropriately, on occasion for other transitional zones. For example, the book by W. Robert Wightman and Nancy M. Wightman, *The Land Between: Northwestern Ontario resource development, 1800 to the 1990s* (University of Toronto Press, 1997), addresses a geographical area totally different from the region described in these essays.

This is not to say that The Land Between of this current book has been neglected, having been represented in whole, or in part, in dozens of publications—popular, academic, and technical—including reports by municipal, provincial, and federal agencies and a number of conservation authorities, but apparently never by name. Numerous journal articles and unpublished papers on specialized subjects lengthen the list, many of which may be traced through the more accessible sources cited below. Many publications include extensive bibliographies, as well as links to a variety of Internet websites. Further publications will be found with the individual authors' biographies recorded elsewhere in this book.

Trent University Library, Trent Valley Archives, Peterborough Public Library, Peterborough Archives, Curve Lake First Nation Office, and Queen's University Library are good starting points for readers wishing to push the subject farther. The periodicals *Journal of Canadian Studies, Ontario History* and *Canadian Geographical Journal* each have carried articles related to The Land Between over the years. The author has deposited a substantial list of relevant books, articles, reports, theses, and manuscripts in each of these institutions.

Alley, Peter. "Could a Significant Natural System in Southern Ontario Be Overlooked?" *Protected Areas and Watershed Management.* Ed. Christopher J. Lemieux, J. Gordon Nelson, Tom J. Beechey, and Michael J. Troughton. Waterloo: Parks Research Forum of Ontario, 2004. 373-83.

Angus, James T. *A Respectable Ditch: a History of the Trent-Severn Waterway, 1833-1920.* Montreal & Kingston: McGill-Queen's University Press, 1988.

Barker, Grace. *Timber Empire: the Exploits of the Entrepreneurial Boyds.* Huntsville: Fox Meadow Creations, 2003.

Barry, James P. *Georgian Bay, the Sixth Great Lake.* 3rd ed. Toronto: Stoddart. 1995.

Blair, Peggy J. *Lament for a First Nation: the Williams Treaties of Southern Ontario.* Vancouver: University of British Columbia Press, 2008.

Bowles, Roy T., R. Brand, and C. Johnston. *Studies of Community Patterns and Planning in the Counties of Peterborough,*

Victoria and Haliburton. Peterborough: Frost Centre for Canadian Heritage and Development Studies, 1986.

Brown, Ron. *Top 115 Unusual Things to See in Ontario*. 3rd ed. Erin: Boston Mills Press, 2012.

Brownell, V. R. and J. L. Riley. *The Alvars of Ontario*. Toronto: Federation of Ontario Naturalists, 2000.

Brunger, Alan G., ed. *Harvey Township: an Illustrated History*. Buckhorn: Greater Harvey Historical Society, 1992.

Cadman, M. D., P. F. J. Eagles, and F. M. Helleiner. *Atlas of the Breeding Birds of Ontario*. Waterloo: University of Waterloo Press, 1987.

Campbell, Claire E. *Shaped by the West Wind: Nature and History in Georgian Bay*. Vancouver: University of British Columbia Press, 2005.

Campbell, John. *The Mazinaw Experience: Bon Echo and Beyond*. Toronto: Natural Heritage Books, 2000.

Capon, Alan R. *Historic Lindsay*. Belleville: Mika Publishing, 1974.

Catling, P. J. and V. J. Brownell. "The flora and ecology of southern Ontario granite barrens," in *Savannas, Barrens and Rock Outcrop Plant Communities of North America*. Edited by R. C. Anderson, J. S. Fralish and J. M. Baskin. Cambridge: Cambridge University Press, 1999.

Chapman, Lyman J., and Donald F. Putnam. *The Physiography of Southern Ontario*. 3rd ed. Toronto: Ontario Ministry of Natural Resources, 1984.

Denison, Merrill. *The Unheroic North: Four Canadian Plays*. Toronto: McClelland & Stewart, 1923.

Fleming, R. B., ed. *The Wartime Letters of Leslie & Cecil Frost, 1915-1919*. Waterloo: Wilfred Laurier University Press, 2007.

Forkey, Neil S. *Shaping the Upper Canadian Frontier: Environment, Society, and Culture in the Trent Valley*. Calgary: University of Calgary Press, 2003.

Frost, Leslie M. *Forgotten Pathways of the Trent*. Don Mills: Burns & MacEachern, 1973.

Gentilcore, R. Louis, and C. Grant Head. *Ontario's History in Maps*. Toronto: University of Toronto Press, 1984.

Gosz, J. R. "Ecotone hierarchies." *Ecological Applications* 3 (1993), 369-76.

Gray, Charlotte. *Sisters in the Wilderness: the Lives of Susanna Moodie and Catharine Parr Traill*. Toronto. Viking, 1999.

Guillet, Edwin C., ed. *The Valley of the Trent*. Toronto: The Champlain Society, 1957.

Hewitt, Donald F. *Geology and Scenery: Peterborough, Bancroft and Madoc Area*. Toronto: Ontario Department of Mines, 1969.

Howe, Clifton D., and James H. White. *Trent Watershed Survey: a Reconnaissance*. Ottawa: Commission of Conservation, 1913.

Irwin, Jane. *Old Canadian Cemeteries: Places of Memory*. Richmond Hill, Ontario: Firefly Books, 2007.

Jones, Elwood H. *A Historian's Notebook: 100 Stories mostly Peterborough*. Peterborough: Trent Valley Archives, 2009.

Jones. L. B. *Living by the Chase: the Native People of Crow and Bobs Lake*. Belleville: Epic Press, 2002.

Killan, Gerald. *Protected Places: a History of Ontario's Provincial Parks System*. Toronto: Dundurn Press, 1993.

Kirkconnell, Watson. *County of Victoria: Centennial History*. 2nd ed. 1921. Lindsay: Victoria County Council, 1967.

Koukkari, Willard, and Robert B. Sothern. *Introducing Biological Rhythms*. New York: Springer, 2006.

Kuhlberg, Mark. *One Hundred Rings and Counting: Forestry Education and Forestry in Toronto and Canada, 1907-2007*. Toronto: University of Toronto Press, 2009.

Landry, Pierre B. *The MacCallum-Jackman Cottage Mural Paintings*. Ottawa: National Gallery of Canada, 1990.

Langman, R. C. *Poverty Pockets: a Study of the Limestone Plains of Southern Ontario*, Toronto: McClelland & Stewart, 1975.

Latimer, John R. *Maker of Men: the Kilcoo Story*. Toronto: John R. Latimer, 1999.

Le Craw, Francis Vernon. *The Land Between: a History of the United Townships of Laxton, Digby and Longford*. published privately, 1967.

Lee, H. T., et al. *Ecological Land Classification for Southern Ontario*. Toronto: Ontario Ministry of Natural Resources, 1998.

Legget, Robert F. *Canals of Canada*. Vancouver: Douglas, David & Charles, 1976.

MacGregor, Rob, et. al. "The Demise of American Eel in the Upper St Lawrence River, Lake Ontario, Ottawa River and Associated Watersheds: Implications of Regional Cumulative Effects in Ontario." *American Fisheries Society Symposium*, 78 (2012), 1-40.

MacKay, Rory. *Spirits of the Little Bonnechere: a History of Exploration, Logging, and Settlement, 1800 to 1920*. Pembroke: Friends of Bonnechere Parks, 1996.

McIlwraith, Thomas F. *Looking for Old Ontario: Two Centuries of Landscape Change*. Toronto: University of Toronto Press, 1997.

Monkman, Drew. *Nature's Year in the Kawarthas: a Guide to the Unfolding Seasons*. Toronto: Dundurn Press, 2002.

Moodie, Susanna. *Life in the Clearings versus the Bush*. 1853. Toronto: Macmillan, 1959.

---. *Roughing It in the Bush, or Forest Life in Canada*. 1852. Toronto: McClelland and Stewart, 1970.

Murray, Florence B. *Muskoka and Haliburton, 1615-1875: a Collection of Documents*. Toronto: Champlain Society, 1963.

Need, Thomas. *Six Years in the Bush, or Extracts from the Journal of a Settler in Upper Canada, 1832-38*. London: Simpkin, Marshall and Company, 1838.

Noss, R. F. and A. Y. Cooperrider. *Saving Nature's Legacy, Protecting and Restoring Biodiversity*. Washington, D. C.: Island Press, 1994.

Osborne, Brian S. "The Kingston Georegion: Going Local in a Globalizing World." *Beyond the Global City: Understanding and Planning for the Diversity of Ontario*. Ed. Gordon Nelson. Montreal and Kingston: McGill-Queen's University Press, 2012, 201-26.

Osborne, Brian S., and Donald Swainson. *Kingston: Building on the Past for the Future*. Kingston: Quarry Press, 2011.

Patterson, William J. *Lilacs and Limestone: an Illustrated History of Pittsburgh Township, 1787-1987*. Kingston: Pittsburgh Historical Society, 1989.

Perrera, Ajith H., David L. Euler, and Ian D. Thompson, eds. *Ecology of a Managed Terrestrial Landscape: Patterns and Processes of Forest Landscapes in Ontario*. Vancouver: University of British Columbia Press, 2000.

Peterman, Michael. *The Great Epoch of Our Lives: Susanna Moodie's "Roughing It in the Bush"*. Toronto: ECW Press, 1996.

---. *Sisters in Two Worlds: a Visual Biography of Susanna Moodie and Catharine Parr Traill*. Toronto: Doubleday Canada, 2007.

Pittaway, Ron. "The Land Between and the Carden Alvar." *Ontario Field Ornithologist News*. Oct. 2007, 17.

Purdy, Al, and Samuel Solecki, eds. *Beyond Remembering: the Collected Poems of Al Purdy*. Madeira Park: Harbour Publishing, 2000.

Raffan, James. *Bark, Skin, and Cedar: Exploring the Canoe in the Canadian Experience*. Toronto: HarperCollins, 1999.

Reid, Ronald and B. Bergsma. *Natural Heritage Evaluation of Muskoka*. Huntsville: District Municipality of Muskoka and the Muskoka Heritage Foundation, 1994.

Rich, Catherine, and Travis Longcore, eds. *Ecological Consequences of Artificial Night Lighting.* Washington: Island Press, 2006.

Riley, J. L.and P. Mohr. *The Natural Heritage of Southern Ontario's Settled Landscapes.* Aurora: Ontario Ministry of Natural Resources, 1994.

Risser, P. G. "Landscape ecology: state of the art," *in Landscapes, Heterogeneity and Disturbance.* Edited by M. Goigel Turner. New York: Springer-Verlag Publishers, 1987.

———. "The status of the science examining ecotones." *Bioscience* 45 (1995), 318-25.

Rollason, Bryan, ed. *County of a Thousand Lakes: the History of the County of Frontenac. 1673-1973.* Kingston: Frontenac County Council, 1982.

Savigny, Mary. *Bon Echo: the Denison Years.* Toronto: Natural Heritage Books, 1997.

Scott, Guy. *History of Kinmount: a Community on the Fringe.* Kinmount: John Deyell Company, 1987.

Sears, Dennis T. Patrick. *The Lark in the Clear Air.* Toronto: McClelland and Stewart, 1974.

Sherman, Paula. *Dishonour of the Crown: the Ontario Resource Regime in the Valley of the Kiji Sibi.* Winnipeg: Arbeiter Ring Publishing, 2008.

Smallwood, P.D., M.A. Steele, and S.H. Faeth. "The Ultimate Basis of the Caching Preferences of Rodents, and the Oak-Dispersal Syndrome: Tannins, Insects, and Seed Germination." *American Zoologist*, 41, 2001, 840-51.

Smith, Donald B. *Sacred Feathers: the Reverend Peter Jones (Kahkewaquonaby) and the Mississauga Indians.* Toronto: University of Toronto Press, 1987.

Tatley, Richard. *Steamboating on the Trent-Severn.* Belleville: Mika Publishing Co., 1978.

Thwaites, Reuben Gold, ed. *The Jesuit Relations and Allied Documents, 1610-1791.* Cleveland: Burrows, 1898. Volume 6, chapter 9, page 309, refers to eels.

Tivy, Louis. *Your Loving Anna: Letters from the Ontario Frontier.* Toronto: University of Toronto Press, 1972.

Traill, Catharine Parr. *The Backwoods of Canada.* 1836. Toronto: Penguin Canada, 2006.

Vastokas, Joan M., and Romas K. Vastokas. *Sacred Art of the Algonkians: a Study of the Peterborough Petroglyphs.* Peterborough: Mansard Press, 1973.

Wadland, John. "Tom Thomson's Places," in Dennis Reid, ed. *Tom Thomson.* Toronto and Ottawa: Art Gallery of Ontario and National Gallery of Canada, 2002, 85-109.

Wall, Geoffrey, and John S. Marsh, eds. *Recreational Land Use: Perspectives on Its Evolution in Canada.* Ottawa: Carleton University Press, 1982.

Wall, Sharon. *The Nurture of Nature: Childhood, Antimodernism, and Ontario Summer Camps, 1920-1955.* Vancouver: University of British Columbia Press, 2009.

Whetung-Derrick, Mae. *History of the Ojibwa of the Curve Lake Reserve and Surrounding Area.* 3 vols. Curve Lake: Curve Lake Indian Band, 1976.

Wightman, William R., and Nancy M. Wightman. *The Land Between: Northwestern Ontario Resource Development, 1800 to the 1990s.* Toronto: University of Toronto Press, 1997.

Williams, Barbara, ed. *A Gentlewoman in Upper Canada: the Journals, Letters and Art of Anne Langton.* Toronto: University of Toronto Press, 2008.

Wood, J. David, ed. *Perspectives on Landscape and Settlement in Nineteenth Century Ontario.* Toronto: McClelland and Stewart Limited, 1975.

CONTRIBUTORS

PETER ALLEY, (1930–2006) a chartered accountant, worked as vice president, finance, of a family company before moving to York University, where for twenty years he taught strategic business management in the MBA program at the Schulich School of Business. Long a summer resident of Muldrew Lake, in 2000 he took up the cause of The Land Between in an active way. He chaired the steering committee that developed The Land Between Collaborative, from which The Land Between Corporation subsequently emerged. DAPHNE ALLEY was primarily the editor and chauffeur for Peter's many trips around the country to teach, recruit, and build an academic base for The Land Between.

DOUG ARMSTRONG, a Torontonian and graduate of University of Guelph, is Professor of Conservation Biology at New Zealand's Massey University in Palmerston North. He specializes in the management of threatened species. He makes regular trips back to the family cottage on the edge of The Land Between, and collaborates with Professor Emeritus Ron Brooks of the University of Guelph on a long-term project involving snapping turtles.

JAMES BARTLEMAN knows The Land Between well. He is a member of the Chippewas of Rama First Nation and has been an astute observer during his lifelong engagement with this region and his people. His thirty-five year career as a Canadian diplomat was followed by his appointment as the first Native Lieutenant Governor of Ontario. Apart from writing biographic volumes on his professional life, James Bartleman has also written several memoirs of his life in Muskoka, as well as fictive accounts loaded with powerful messages about his people.

NATHAN BASILIKO is Associate Professor at the Vale "Living with Lakes" Centre and the Department of Biology at Laurentian University. He was formerly a member of the Department of Geography at the University of Toronto, Mississauga. He is a soil scientist with a research focus on the forests and wetlands of central and northern Ontario and the impact of environmental changes on these ecosystems.

LEORA BERMAN, originally from southern Africa, became acquainted with Ontario by visiting each First Nation reserve and provincial park. She studied English and Economics at McMaster University, and Environmental Technology at Sir Sandford Fleming College. She has led and developed a regional stewardship program for The Land Between since 2006, building on her commitment to the interplay of culture, ecology, and resource management.

ROY T. BOWLES is Professor Emeritus of Sociology at Trent University. Since 1969 he has lived near Lakefield, in the southerly part of The Land Between. Hiking, canoeing, and driving through this region have been sources of pleasure and insight for forty years. His studies and writing focused on small Canadian communities, especially those based on resource industries.

RON BROWN is a freelance travel writer, and author of more than twenty books highlighting forgotten heritage features of Canada and Ontario. Subjects include ghost towns, railways, and unusual destinations. His titles include *The Top 100 Unusual Things to See in Ontario* (2007) and *In Search of the Grand Trunk: Ghost Rail Lines in Ontario* (2010). He is a past Chair of the Writers' Union of Canada.

ALAN G. BRUNGER is Professor Emeritus of Geography at Trent University. He has undertaken research on the European settlement of Peterborough County and Kawartha Lakes region. He edited the local heritage guide *By Lake and Lock* (1985) and *Harvey Township: An Illustrated History* (1992). He is pursuing further research interests in 19th century Ontario settlement.

CLAIRE ELIZABETH CAMPBELL is Associate Professor at Dalhousie University, where she teaches in History, Canadian Studies, and the College of Sustainability. Although she now lives on another shoreline, she remains inspired by her early years spent in the Georgian Bay archipelago. She is author of *Shaped by the West Wind: Nature and History in Georgian Bay* (2005), and editor of *A Century of Parks Canada, 1911-2011* (2011).

DUGALD M. CARMICHAEL fell in love with the bedrock geology of The Land Between as a freshman field-tripper at Queen's University in 1957. Later, The Land Between provided him with a B.Sc. thesis research area in what is now Frontenac Park, a Ph.D. thesis area in west-central Hastings County, a matchless venue for leading geological field trips while teaching geology at Queen's for thirty-one years, and forty years (so far) of exuberant white water paddling and off-trail hiking, skiing, and snowshoeing.

DENNIS CARTER-EDWARDS is Cultural Resource Specialist for the Trent-Severn Waterway National Historic Sites Commission and formerly research historian with Parks Canada. Active in commemorating Ontario's heritage, he is a former Chair of the Preservation Committee for The Ontario Historical Society and is currently President of the Peterborough Historical Society. He has written extensively on Ontario's military history and is developing a heritage network for the Trent-Severn Waterway.

ROBERT DICK is a mechanical and spacecraft engineer, astronomer and, now it seems, an environmentalist. He taught astronomy and engineering at two universities for a total of twenty-five years. He developed the National Light Pollution Abatement Program for the Royal Astronomical Society of Canada and the Canadian Dark Sky Preserve Program for national and provincial parks. His goal is to leave the world a better place.

RORY ECKENSWILLER is a graduate of Trent University and currently Manager of the Algonquin Wildlife Research Station, founded in 1944 on Lake Sasajewun in Algonquin Park.

The publications of **RAE B. FLEMING** deal with a wide range of topics, from Canadian general stores to Sir William Mackenzie, the Royal Tour of 1939, and World War I letters written by the Frost brothers, Cecil and Leslie. Fleming's articles have appeared in Canada's history and academic journals. In 2010 he published *Peter Gzowski: A Biography*. That year Fleming was awarded a Lieutenant Governor's Ontario Heritage Award for Lifetime Achievement.

NEIL S. FORKEY teaches in the Canadian Studies Department at St. Lawrence University. He is author of *Shaping the Upper Canadian Frontier: Environment, Society, and Culture in the Trent Valley* (2003). His work has appeared in the *Journal of Canadian Studies*, *The Canadian Historical Review*, *Ontario History*, and *Forest and Conservation History*. He is currently writing a Canadian environmental history survey text for the University of Toronto Press.

JANE IRWIN (1941-2013) taught English Literature at Trent University for eleven years before retiring to take up full-time research on local history and heritage conservation. She was a life member of the Ontario Historical Society and author of *Old Canadian Cemeteries: Places of Memory* (2007).

GORDON JOHNSTON has been teaching and writing about Canadian Poetry at Trent University for forty years, and has been particularly interested in the relation of poems to their locations. He is a poet himself, having published *Small Wonder* (2006) and *Advancing Stranger* (2007). His current scholarly work is on the Confederation poet, Archibald Lampman, who knew a thing or two about The Land Between.

ELWOOD H. JONES is Professor Emeritus of History at Trent University and archivist at Trent Valley Archives and St. John's Anglican Church. He writes a Saturday column, "Historian at Work," for the *Peterborough Examiner* and edits *Heritage Gazette of the Trent Valley*. His dozen books on Peterborough history include *Winners: 150 Years of the Peterborough Exhibition* (1995), *Fighting Fires in Peterborough* (2008), *An Historian's Notebook* (2009), and *Little Lake Cemetery* (2010).

LOUISE LIVINGSTONE, originally from Oxford, UK, studied ecological sciences, environmental planning, and journalism at the University of Edinburgh, Heriot Watt University, and Loyalist College. She taught at Aberdeen University, Robert Gordon University, Queen's University, and Loyalist College and has worked as a planner, journalist, and photographer. She coordinates the sustainable agriculture project, Harvest Hastings, and is a member of the Deloro Mine Site Cleanup Public Liaison Committee.

NIK LUKA is on the faculty of the Schools of Architecture and Urban Planning at McGill University in Montréal, where he coordinates the graduate program in Urban Design. Hailing from Toronto, he has long family histories in The Land Between and central Québec; he also grew up summering on Georgian Bay and in central Haliburton. His work encompasses changing landscapes, representations, and mediations of urban space, housing, cottage life, and infrastructure as public space.

JOHN S. MARSH is Professor Emeritus of Geography at Trent University where he directs the Trail Studies Unit and continues research on conservation, tourism, and heritage. He has become familiar with The Land Between by lobbying for and cycling its rail trails, canoeing the Pigeon River, camping in Kawartha Highlands, swimming in Chemung Lake, taking photos of old barns and farmhouses, going to Bigley's for shoes and Lakefield for ice cream.

LAUREL SEFTON MacDOWELL, Professor of History at the University of Toronto, studies Canadian working-class history and North American environmental history. Her books include *Remember Kirkland Lake: The Gold Miners' Strike of 1941-42* (2001), *Renegade Lawyer: The Life of J. L. Cohen* (2001), and *An Environmental History of Canada* (2012). As a child she cottaged in the Kawartha Lakes; she resides in Toronto and Haliburton.

ROBERT B. MacGREGOR is a fisheries biologist, retired from the Ontario Ministry of Natural Resources. For fully a decade he has focused on the science, management, conservation, and recovery strategy of the American Eel in Lake Ontario and adjacent waters. He has published widely on this subject, and has spoken frequently to both professional and public audiences on fish management issues.

BARBARA McFADZEN joined the A. Sheila Boyd Foundation in Bobcaygeon in 1992 and was its Chair from 1994 to 2010. During her tenure the Boyd Heritage Museum opened to the public; it is situated at Lock 32 on the Trent-Severn Waterway in the original 1889 business offices of the Mossom Boyd Lumber Company. She is currently Vice-chair and a continuing Director of the Museum. Other interests involve dogs, bicycles, art, gardens, and more.

THOMAS F. McILWRAITH is a semi-retired Geographer at the University of Toronto, Mississauga. He is author of *Looking for Old Ontario* (1997), and co-editor of *North America: The Historical Geography of a Changing Continent* (2001). He has been active in heritage conservation in Mississauga, recently retired as book review editor of *Ontario History*, and is currently writing a cultural and technological history of Ontario railways.

RICHARD B. MILLER (1915–1959) was a wildlife biologist at the University of Alberta specializing in fish ecology; a research station in the Canadian Rockies is named after him. He spent childhood summers on Georgian Bay, and worked on his Ph. D. in Algonquin Park during summers in the 1930s. In 1944 he revisited his parents' summer place on Georgian Bay, an occasion that stimulated lines later published in *A Cool Curving World*.

BRIAN S. OSBORNE, Professor Emeritus at Queen's University, has known The Land Between since 1967. The Frontenac Arch has bulked large in his many studies of the settlement history, development, and perception of the Kingston region. As a canoeist, he has traversed its extent along the Madawaska, the Mississippi, and Rideau-Cataraqui systems. As a cottager on Brule Lake for four decades, he considers himself to be a resident of The Land Between.

JOHN PARRY has been copy editing scholarly books for over thirty years and in 2010 set up Words Indeed Publishing Inc. He has prepared a collection of "book stories" about his professional life and has written about his family, who started spending summers in Georgian Bay 130 years ago.

MICHÈLE PROULX, a planner for Ontario Parks, lives in Thunder Bay with her dog Ruby and cat Chicken. She first became aware of uranium in The Land Between during the 1980s while working in the Ministry of Natural Resources Junior Ranger Program at Bancroft. A graduate of Trent University, she undertook research into the untold story of uranium in Haliburton County. The rest is environmental history.

AL (ALFRED WELLINGTON) PURDY (1918–2000), grew up in rural Northumberland County, on the edge of The Land Between. He was author of more than thirty books of poetry, as well as other literary works. He was recipient of the Order of Ontario and the Order of Canada. In his later years he divided his time between Vancouver Island and his cottage at Roblin Lake in Prince Edward County.

JAMES RAFFAN, Executive Director of the Canadian Canoe Museum in Peterborough, has written extensively about Canada's boreal regions and canoeing. He is past chair of the Arctic Institute of North America, and a former governor of the Royal Canadian Geographical Society, service for which he was awarded the Queen's Jubilee Medal in 2002. A restless traveller, he is nevertheless always delighted to return to his home in The Land Between north of Kingston.

RON REID resides in Washago, in the heart of The Land Between. He has spent his career studying and protecting natural heritage, particularly on the Carden limestone plain and in Muskoka. In recent years he was Executive Director for The Couchiching Conservancy, a regional land trust, and now serves as Carden Program Coordinator, where he has helped assemble a protected land base of over 8,000 acres (about 3,200 hectares).

TARA SACKETT is a post-doctoral research associate at the University of Toronto, and her research explores the links between invertebrate communities and forest ecosystem processes. Her studies of exotic earthworms at Haliburton Forest provided the initial impetus for first visiting The Land Between in 2010, but these trips quickly grew to include The Land Between as a favourite location for camping and canoeing.

GUY SCOTT, a high-school history teacher from Kinmount, is a fifth generation rock farmer on the family farm in Galway Township. Specializing in the history of agricultural fairs, his books include *Country Fairs in Canada* (2006), *Ontario Agricultural Fairs: A Snapshot in Time* (2008) and, much earlier, *A History of Kinmount* (1988). He has arranged bus tours, walking tours, and engaged in public speaking and old-fashioned storytelling. His latest project involves the Kinmount *Gazette*, a historical newspaper.

JOHN WADLAND lives in Peterborough and taught at Trent University for thirty-six years. Before his retirement in 2008 he served as Editor of the *Journal of Canadian Studies*, Chair of the undergraduate Canadian Studies Program, and Director of the Frost Centre for Canadian Studies and Indigenous Studies. He has a special interest in interdisciplinary research and pedagogy, most of which has focused on environmental themes.

MURRAY WHETUNG is an Anishnaabeg Elder of Curve Lake First Nation. Following service as a signaler in World War II, for which he was decorated, Murray has been a mechanic and farmer, and always a crack shot. He entered the ministry of the United Church of Canada during the 1980s. He is a founder of a ministerial school for First Nations, and began the All Native Conference.

TOM WHILLANS is a professor at Trent University in the Environmental and Resource Studies Program. He has been working in The Land Between since 1974, when he joined the aquatic research project at the Royal Ontario Museum's field station near Bobcaygeon. He had been primed by research in the Northwest Territories Land Between. His research and development activities have focused on the lower Great Lakes, Haliburton, Anishinabek communities, and the Ecuadorian Sierra.

DANA H. WILSON is Assistant Professor in the School of Rural and Northern Health at Laurentian University, and taught previously at the University of Toronto Mississauga. She is a health geographer with interests in social inequalities in health, neighbourhood conditions, and local opportunities for youth development. Having grown up in Wasaga Beach just shy of the western limits of The Land Between, she has a keen interest in the area.

ACKNOWLEDGEMENTS

The Land Between Circle gratefully acknowledges financial support from the following institutions:

- The Frost Centre for Canadian Studies and Indigenous Studies, Trent University, Peterborough.
- The Symons Trust for Canadian Studies, Trent University, Peterborough.
- The Trillium Foundation, Ontario.
- The Land Between, Incorporated.

We acknowledge these institutions and individuals for granting permission to use their materials:

- Library and Archives Canada, for correspondence between A.Y. Jackson and Anne Savage, used by Claire Elizabeth Campbell in "Love letters from the Western Islands." Anne Savage fonds, A.Y. Jackson correspondence, MG30-D374 (old reference) or R5476-0-8-E (new reference).
- Don LePan, administrator for Douglas LePan, for quoting the lines from his father's poem, "Islands of Summer," used by Claire Elizabeth Campbell in "Remembering Camp Hurontario."
- Rives Dalley Hewitt, Amy Grant, Edward Irvine, David Latimer, and Janet Zimmerman, for assistance in preparation of "Independence and Freedom: Sibelius and Lismer" by John Parry.
- Harbour Publishing, for quoting "The Country North of Belleville" by Al Purdy, in "Al Purdy's Back Country" by Gordon Johnston.
- Musée national des beaux-arts du Québec, for reproducing Otto Reinhold Jacobi and Adolf Vogt "Vue de la Mississippi, vallée de l'Outaouais," in "Imagining the Land Between with Otto Jacobi" by Brian S. Osborne.
- National Gallery of Canada, for reproducing Arthur Lismer "The Skinny Dip," in "Independence and Freedom: Sibelius and Lismer" by John Parry.
- National Gallery of Canada, for reproducing A.Y. Jackson "Boat and Tent at Night, Western Islands," in "Love letters from the Western Islands" by Claire Elizabeth Campbell.

Photographs that accompany individual essays have been provided by the respective authors, unless noted otherwise. Unattributed photographs have been provided by The Land Between and the Ontario Visual Heritage Project; these appear on pages 1, 4, 6, 12, 20, 22, 25, 35, 37 (Ivan Kmit/Photos.com), 52, 55, 59 (kamranm/Photos.com), 61, 67, 76 (Kerry Plumley), 79, 82, 88, 91 (Elana Elisseeva/Photos.com), 99, 100, 100, 101, 109, 119, 124, 130, 133, 139, 145, 151, 154, 156. Maps on pages 16, 96, 121 courtesy of Dugald Carmichael. The publisher welcomes information on illustrations for which attribution is incomplete or incorrect.